SRA
Reading Mastery®
Transformations

Reading
Workbook A

Siegfried Engelmann

Susan Hanner

McGraw Hill

Acknowledgments

The authors are extremely grateful to Tina Wells for keeping the ship afloat on this project, and to Patricia McFadden, Margie Mayo, and Chris Gladfelter for their great attention to detail.

PHOTO CREDITS
046 (tl)Amazon-Images/Alamy Stock Photo, (tc)Mark Morgan/Alamy Stock Photo, (tr)WeatherVideoHD.TV;
056 (l)Mark Morgan/Alamy Stock Photo, (c)Amazon-Images/Alamy Stock Photo, (r)WeatherVideoHD.TV.

mheducation.com/prek-12

Copyright © 2021 McGraw-Hill Education

Send all inquiries to:
McGraw-Hill Education
8787 Orion Place
Columbus, OH 43240

ISBN: 978-0-07-905368-8
MHID: 0-07-905368-8

Printed in the United States of America.

1 2 3 4 5 6 7 8 9 LOV 24 23 22 21 20

A INFORMATION ITEMS

1. What's the name of geese that are all white?

   _____

2. What's the name of geese that are black, brown, and white?

   _____

3. Both geese and ducks are water birds, but _____ are a lot bigger.

4. You can tell male geese from female geese because ▮▮▮▮ .
   • male geese have brighter colors
   • male geese are larger
   • male geese have longer feathers

5. What color are all geese when they are born?

   _____

6. How old are geese when they mate for the first time?

   _____

7. After male and female geese mate, they stay together ▮▮▮▮ .
   • for the summer
   • for a full year
   • until one goose dies

B STORY ITEMS

1. Most geese live for about _____ years.

2. How old was Old Henry?

   _____

3. What was the name of the lake where the flock lived during the summer?

   _____

4. In which season did the flock leave the lake?
   • spring
   • summer
   • fall
   • winter

5. In which direction did the flock fly?
   • north
   • south
   • east
   • west

6. How far was the flock going?

   _____

7. Who didn't want to make the trip?

   _____

8. He said that he was too _____ to fly so far.

9. What will happen to Big Trout Lake during the winter?

   _____

END OF LESSON 1

2   Lesson 1

A INFORMATION ITEMS

1. Make an **R** on Big Trout Lake.

2. What country is the **R** in?

   _____

3. Make an **F** on Crooked Lake.

4. Which lake is farther north?

   _____

5. Make a **Y** next to the lake that freezes in the winter.

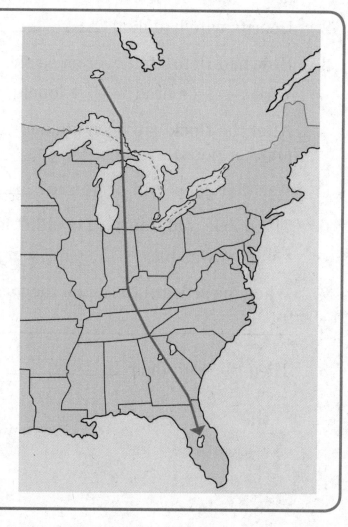

6. Geese live in large groups called _____.

7. In what country are most wild geese born? _____

8. Where do these geese spend every summer? _____

9. In which direction do the geese fly in the fall? _____

10. What is this trip called?
    • mating   • migration   • vacation

11. Why do the geese leave Canada in the fall?
    • There is no snow.   • The lakes freeze.   • The flock needs to fly.

12. Every fall, Old Henry's flock went to the state of _____.

1. Henry first mated with his wife when they were both _____ years old.

2. Henry's wife had died _____ years ago.

3. How had Henry felt ever since she had died?
   • free   • tired   • lonely

4. After the flock had been gone for _____ days, Henry saw another goose.

5. Was that goose **old** or **young?** _____

6. The goose told Henry, "I couldn't learn to fly because ▮▮▮▮ ."
   • my leg was hurt   • my wing was hurt   • I was too small

7. When geese learn to fly, do they start **in the water** or **on the land?**

   _____

8. They run with their _____ out to the sides.

GO TO PART D IN YOUR TEXTBOOK

A INFORMATION ITEMS

1. Write the directions **north, south, east,** and **west** in the boxes on map 1.

2. In which direction do geese migrate in the fall? _____

3. In which direction do geese migrate in the spring? _____

4. Make a line that starts at the circle on the map and goes north.

5. If you start at the circle and move to the number **4,** in which direction do you go? _____

Map 1

Look at map 2 on the next page.

6. What country is the **A** in? _____

7. What country is the **B** in? _____

8. What **state** is the **B** in? _____

9. If you started at the **B** and went to the **A,** in which direction would you go? _____

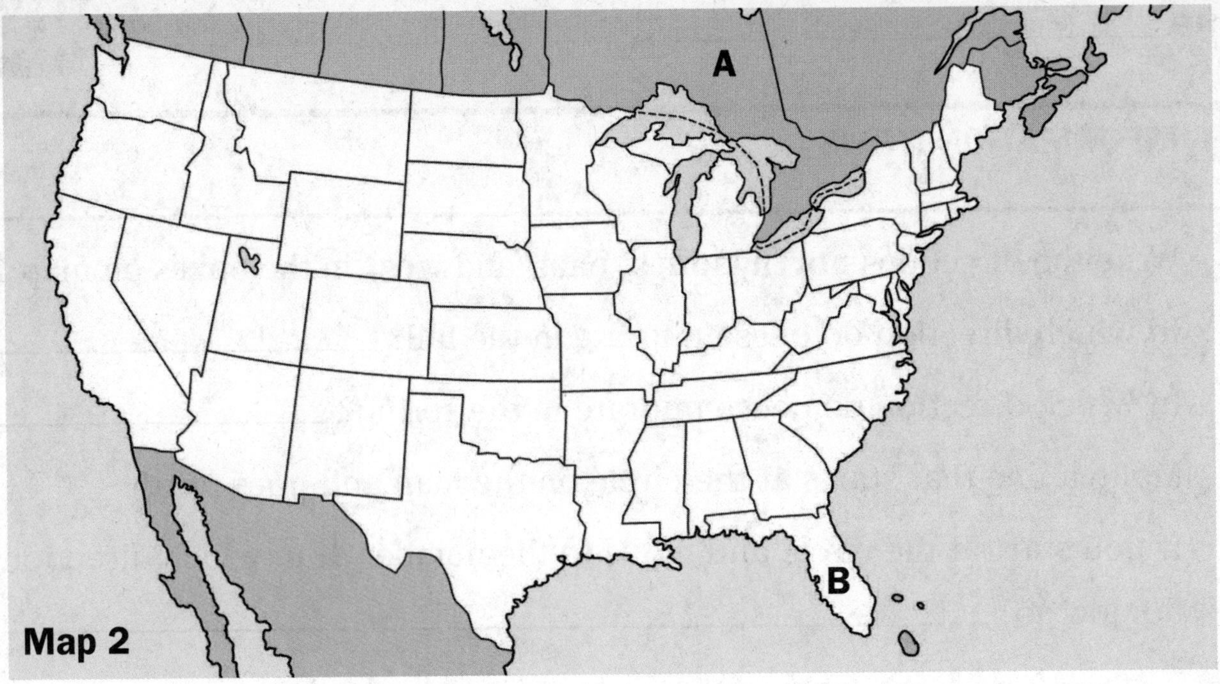

B STORY ITEMS

1. What was the name of the young goose? ______________________

2. When was that goose born? ______________________

3. How old was he?
   - more than a year
   - less than half a year
   - more than half a year

4. When young geese learn to fly, they hold their wings out as they ______.
   - walk
   - run
   - swim

5. Tim couldn't learn to fly because he couldn't ______________________.

6. Was his leg still hurt? ______________________

7. Circle the 2 things that Henry said he would do for Tim.
   - show him how to stay warm
   - build a warm house for him
   - fly with him to Florida
   - tell him how to get to Florida
   - teach him how to fly

GO TO PART D IN YOUR TEXTBOOK

A **INFORMATION ITEMS**

Look at the map below.

1. What's the name of the place shown by the letter **A**? _____

2. Which letter shows the coldest place? _____

3. Which letter shows the hottest place? _____

4. Which letter is farthest from the equator? _____

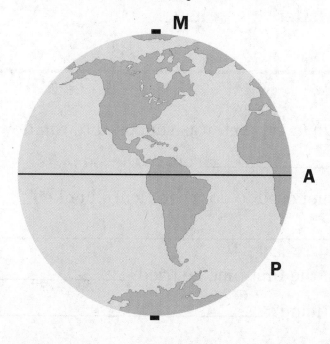

5. The earth is shaped like a _____ .

6. The hottest part of the earth is called the ▮▮▮ .

   • pole   • desert   • equator

7. What's the name of the line that goes around the fattest part of the earth?

   _____

8. What's the name of the spot that's at the top of the earth?

   _____

9. What's the name of the spot that's at the bottom of the earth?

   _____

10. The _____s are the coldest places on the earth and the

    _____ is the hottest place on the earth.

11. How many poles are there? _____

12. Are the equator and the poles **real marks** on the earth or **pretend marks?**

    _____

13. The farther you go from the equator, the ▮▮▮▮▮ it gets.
    • colder   • fatter   • hotter

B STORY ITEMS

1. Henry taught Tim to fly. Tim was supposed to run down _____

   and hold his _____ out to the side.

2. What was Tim supposed to do when Henry honked?

   _____

3. Did Tim take off the first time he tried? _____

4. Did he keep on flying? _____

5. Why? _____

6. Did Tim do better the second time he tried? _____

7. How high did the geese fly? _____

8. Where did they land? _____

9. Who was going too fast when they landed? _____

GO TO PART D IN YOUR TEXTBOOK

A INFORMATION ITEMS

Choose from these words to answer each item:

- moon
- poles
- Florida
- Canada
- equator
- migration
- geese
- sun

1. The heat that the earth receives comes from the _____ .

2. The part of the earth that receives more heat than any other part is the _____ .

3. The parts of the earth that receive less heat than any other part are called the _____ .

B STORY ITEMS

1. How many days did Tim practice flying? _____

2. When Tim flew in the direction that felt best, in which direction did he fly? _____

3. How much of the lake was frozen by the end of the third day that Tim practiced?
   - almost all
   - half
   - all

4. How much of the lake did Henry think would be frozen by the next morning? _____

5. Was Tim able to understand what Henry explained about the landing places? _____

6. How many landing places are there on the trip to Florida? _____

7. The first landing place is a field next to a _____ .

8. That landing place has _____ on it.

SKILL ITEMS

The horses became restless on the dangerous route.

1. What word tells you about how you get to a place? _____

2. What word tells how you feel when you want to do something different? _____

D **REVIEW ITEMS**

1. In which direction do geese fly in the fall? _____

2. What is this trip called? _____

3. In which direction do geese fly in the spring? _____

4. Write the directions **north, south, east,** and **west** in the boxes.

5. Make a line that starts at the circle on the map and goes east.

6. If you start at the circle and move to the number **3,** in which direction do you go? _____

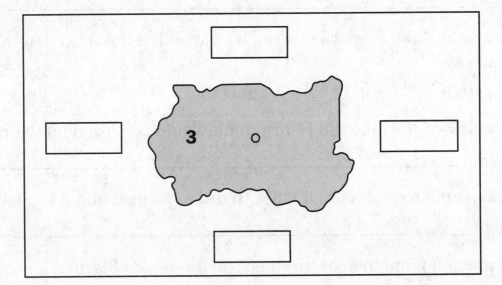

GO TO PART D IN YOUR TEXTBOOK

Name _____

A INFORMATION ITEMS

1. The sun shines ▮▮▮▮ .
    - some of the time   - all of the time

2. Can you see the sun all day long and all night long? _____

3. If you can see the sun, you are on the side of the earth that is ▮▮▮▮ .
    - closer to the sun   - farther from the sun

4. If you can see the sun, it is ▮▮▮▮ on your side of the earth.
    - nighttime   - daytime

5. What is it on the other side of the earth? _____

Look at the picture.

6. Shade the part of the earth where it is nighttime.

7. Which side of the earth is closer to the sun, A or B? _____

8. Which side of the earth is in nighttime? _____

9. Which side of the earth is in daytime? _____

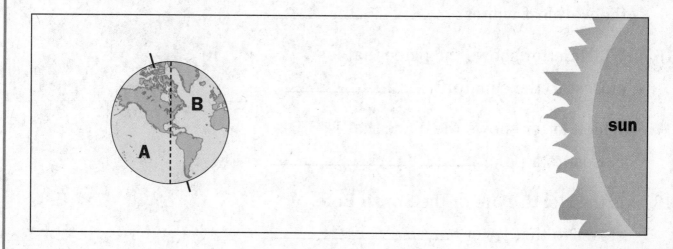

---

10. The earth turns around one time every _____ hours.

11. Write the letter of the earth that shows the person in daytime. _____

12. Write the letter of the earth that shows the person 6 hours later. _____

13. Write the letter that shows the person another 6 hours later.

_____

14. Write the letter that shows the person another 6 hours later.

_____

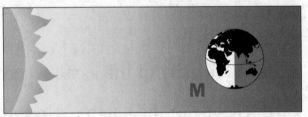

15. Which letter shows the place that has the warmest winter? _____

16. Which letter shows the place that is closest to the equator? _____

17. Which letter shows the place that is closest to a pole? _____

18. Is the **North Pole** or the **South Pole** closer to that letter? _____

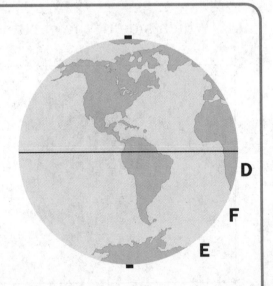

GO TO PART D IN YOUR TEXTBOOK

Name ______________________________

A INFORMATION ITEMS

1. Which letter on the map shows Big Trout Lake? __________
2. Which letter shows the landing place in Kentucky? __________
3. Which letter shows the landing place in Michigan? __________
4. Which letter shows the landing place in Florida? __________
5. Which letter shows the landing place in Canada? __________
6. Which letter shows Crooked Lake? __________
7. Which letter shows the first landing place? __________
8. Which letter shows the second landing place? __________
9. Draw the path the geese take on their migration south.

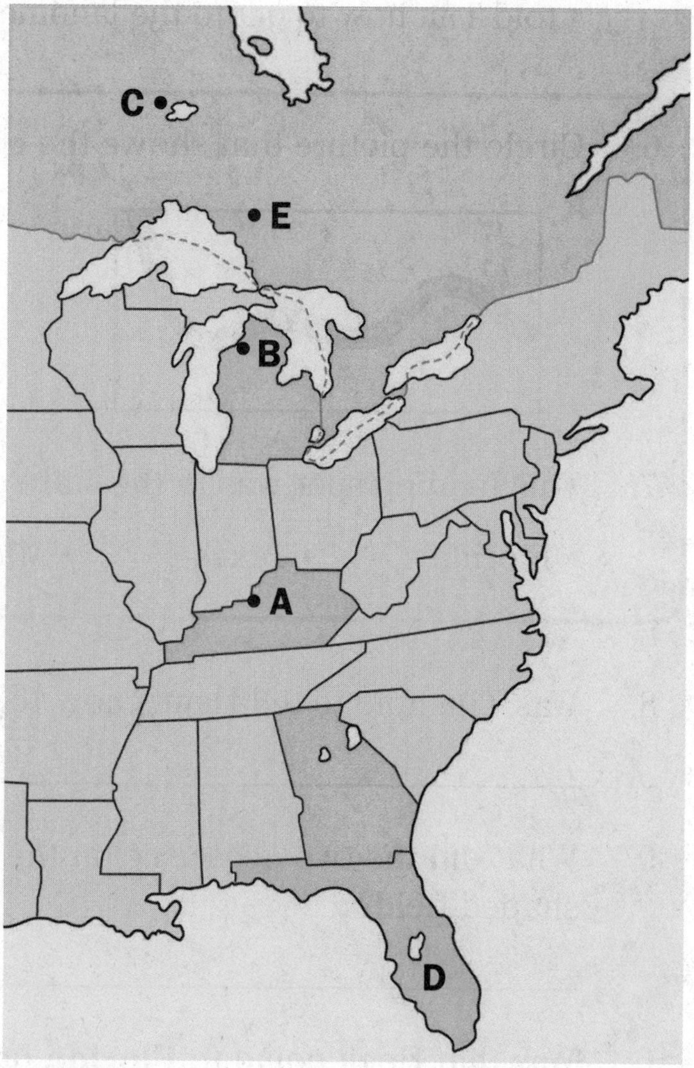

B STORY ITEMS

1. Did Henry tell Tim about his sore wing? __________
2. He got a sore wing when he fought with __________.
3. Henry told Tim about the next landing place. He also made a ▬▬.
   - mess
   - map
   - story

4. Did Tim recognize the next landing spot? _____

5. So what did Henry do?
   - led Tim to the landing place
   - told Tim how to get to the landing place

6. Circle the picture that shows the correct landing spot.

   A 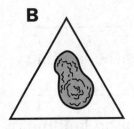   **B**   **C**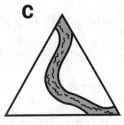

7. This landing spot was in the state of ▮▮▮▮ .
   - Florida   • Texas   • Michigan

8. Was Tim able to tell Henry how to get back to the first landing place?

   _____

9. What did the two geese see on the second day they were at the triangle-shaped field?

   _____

10. Was that flock going to **Florida** or **Mexico?** _____

11. When Tim and Henry left Big Trout Lake, Henry had planned to take Tim to the first _____ landing places.

12. Now Henry realized that somebody would have to fly farther with Tim. How far? _____

13. Was Henry sure that he would be able to fly that far with Tim? _____

GO TO PART D IN YOUR TEXTBOOK

A STORY ITEMS

1. How many Great Lakes are there? _____

2. Color the Great Lakes on the map.

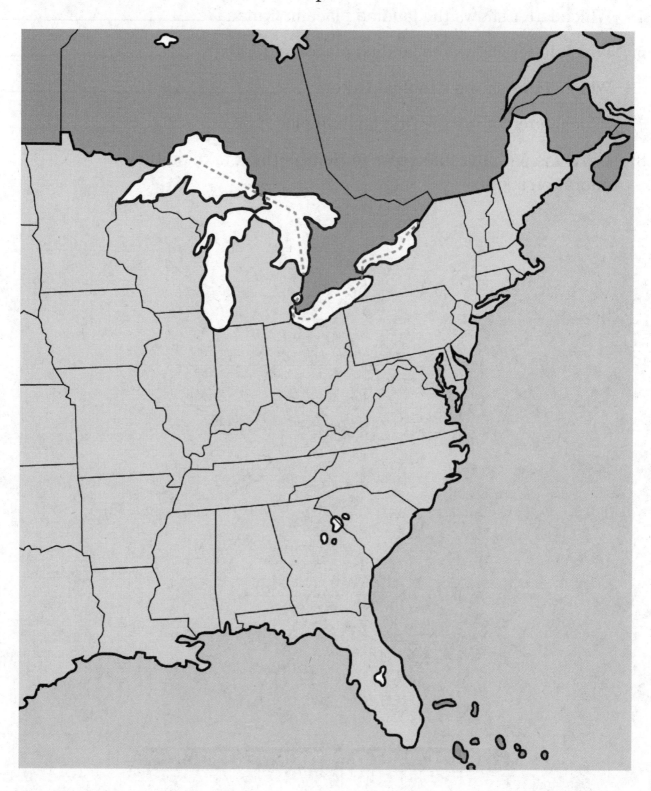

1. Which letter on the map below shows the landing place in Kentucky? _____

2. Which letter shows Big Trout Lake? _____

3. Which letter shows the landing place in Michigan? _____

4. Which letter shows the landing place in Canada? _____

5. Which letter shows the landing place in Florida? _____

6. Which letter shows Crooked Lake? _____

7. Which letter shows the first landing place? _____

8. Draw the path that the geese in Henry's flock take on their migration south.

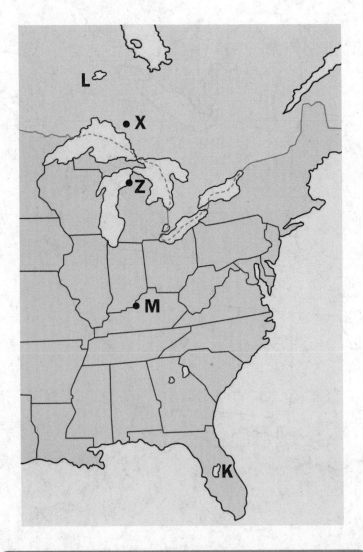

GO TO PART D IN YOUR TEXTBOOK

A   INFORMATION ITEMS

1. The earth makes a circle around the sun one time every ▮▮▮ .

    • hour   • day   • year

2. How many days does it take the earth to make one full circle around
    the sun? _____

3. **Fill in the blanks to show the four seasons.**

    winter, _____ , summer, fall, _____ ,
    spring, _____ , _____

4. Write the missing seasons on the picture below.

5. Shade half of earth A and half of earth C.

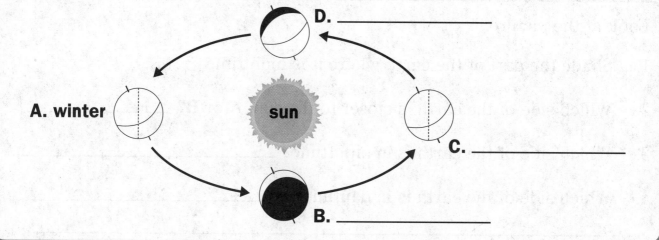

B   STORY ITEMS

1. When Tim and Henry were in Kentucky, did Henry want to fly farther
    south? _____

2. Tim said he'd fly with the flock if Henry _____ .

3. Was it **easier** or **harder** to fly with the large flock? _____

4. Were Tim and Henry **near** or **far** from the point of the V? _____

5. Flying near the back of a large flock is like riding your bike [____] .

   • with the wind   • against the wind

6. Look at the picture. Write **H** on the goose that has to work the hardest.

7. Color the air that is moving in the same direction the flock is moving.

C REVIEW ITEMS

Look at the picture.

1. Shade the part of the earth where it is nighttime.

2. Which side of the earth is closer to the sun, **A** or **B**? _____

3. Which side of the earth is in nighttime? _____

4. Which side of the earth is in daytime? _____

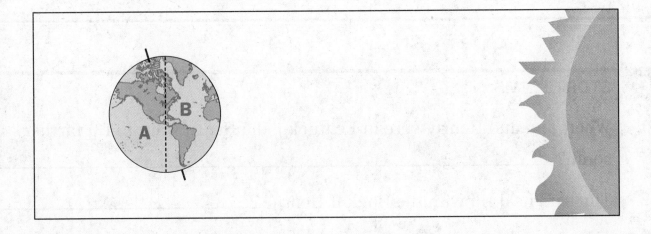

5. How many Great Lakes are there? _____

6. Color the Great Lakes on the map.

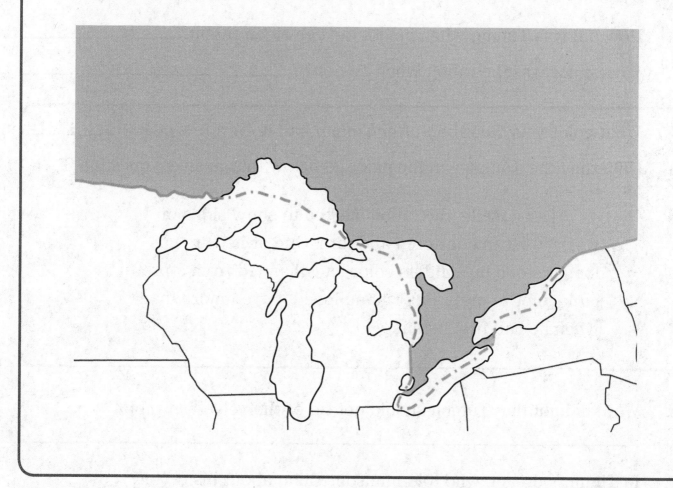

GO TO PART D IN YOUR TEXTBOOK

A   STORY ITEMS

1.   How old was Timmy when he got the velveteen rabbit? _____

2.   What color was the rabbit when he got it? _____

3.   What color was the rabbit after Timmy had it for a few years? _____

4.   Underline the sentence in the passage below that answers question 3.

> After a while, the rabbit started to show signs of
> wear. It became tattered and torn. One of its ears no
> longer stood up. And its color had changed from a pretty
> pink color to gray. But Timmy loved it even more than
> when he had first held it.

5.   Who thought that Timmy should get rid of the velveteen rabbit?

_____

6.   In Timmy's dream, who told him something about his rabbit?

_____

7.   What did that person say would happen to the rabbit?

_____

8.   Where did his mother tell him to take the tattered rabbit?

_____

9.   When Timmy looked back at the rabbit, how had it changed?

_____

All stories have three main elements. They are the **setting,** the **characters,** and the **plot.**

- The **setting** is where and when the story takes place.
- The **characters** are the important people, animals, or objects that do things in the story.
- The **plot** is what happens to the characters in the story.

Answer these questions.

1. What is the setting for the beginning of the story?

    _____

2. Name the two main characters in this story.

    _____

3. Write the letter of the passage that tells the **plot** for this story. _____

    A. A boy named Timmy got sick. A princess told Timmy that his velveteen rabbit was her friend. When Timmy was older, his mother put the rabbit in the woods. She thought Timmy was too big to have a toy rabbit.

    B. Timmy's favorite toy was a stuffed velveteen rabbit. A princess told him it was real. Timmy's mother didn't like the toy rabbit, so she bought Timmy a real rabbit. Timmy liked the real rabbit so much that he forgot all about his old stuffed toy.

    C. Timmy's favorite toy was a stuffed velveteen rabbit. Timmy loved the rabbit. When Timmy got sick, loving the rabbit helped him get better. When Timmy was older, he left the rabbit in the woods. When he looked back, there was a live rabbit right where he had left his toy.

END OF LESSON 10

Name _____

1. Write the number of the earth that has the North Pole tilting away from the sun. _____

2. Write the number of the earth that has the North Pole tilting toward the sun. _____

3. During which season is there darkness all around the North Pole?

    _____

4. During which season is there daylight all around the North Pole?

    _____

Write which season each earth in the picture shows.

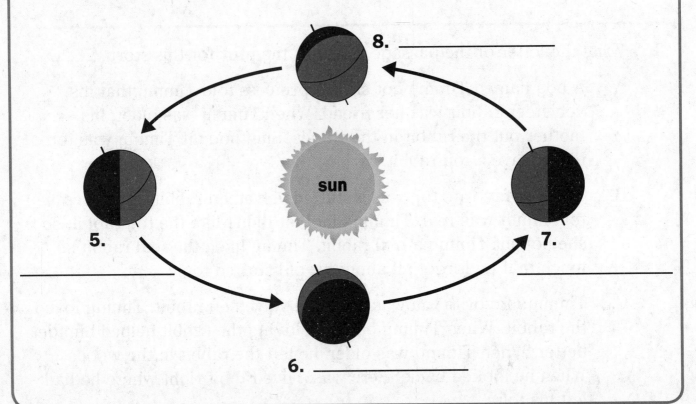

8. _____

5. _____

sun

7. _____

6. _____

9. The picture shows the sun and two balls. **Fix up the balls so that half of each ball is in the sunlight and half is in shadow.**

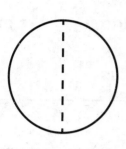  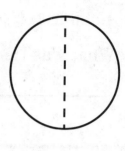

sun

10. During winter at the North Pole, how often does the sun shine?

    • never   • all the time

11. During summer at the North Pole, how often does the sun shine?

    • never   • all the time

12. What season is it at the North Pole when the North Pole tilts **toward** the sun? _____

13. What season is it at the North Pole when the North Pole tilts **away from** the sun? _____

B STORY ITEMS

1. In today's chapter, the flock started out at Jackson Lake in the state of _____ .

2. The flock landed at Newnans Lake in the state of _____ .

3. The flock rested for _____ days.

4. Then the flock flew to _____ Lake in the state of _____ .

5. The flock they were flying with went on to _____ Lake.

6. Circle the geese Tim was looking forward to seeing.

   • children   • friends   • dad   • grandchildren   • mom

7. Circle the geese Henry was looking forward to seeing.

   • children   • friends   • dad   • grandchildren   • mom

8. What was Henry going to miss?

   _____

C REVIEW ITEMS

1. Write **H** on the goose in the picture that works the hardest.

2. Color the air that is moving in the same direction the flock is moving.

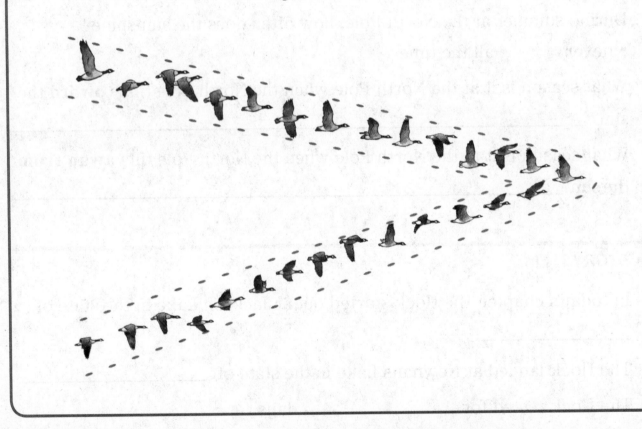

A | **INFORMATION ITEMS**

1. Which letter on the map shows Alaska? _____

2. Which letter shows the main part of the United States? _____

3. Which letter shows Canada? _____

4. Which 2 letters show where Inuits live? _____ and _____

5. How warm is it during winter in Alaska? _____

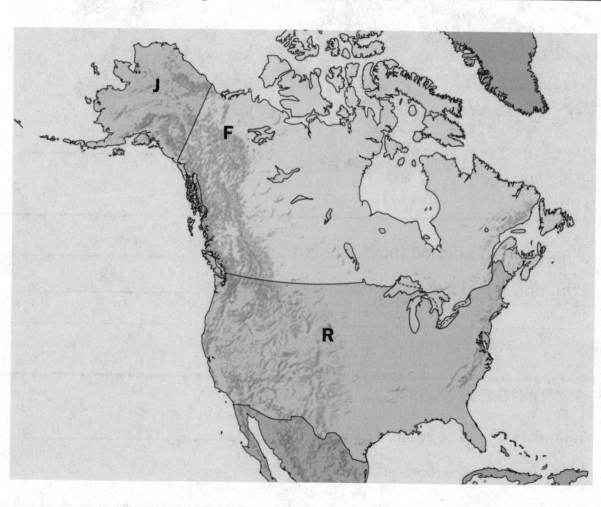

Look at the picture below. **Write the name of these objects in the correct place:**

- parka
- fishing pole
- sled
- sled dogs
- fishing spear
- kayak

6. _____

7. _____

8. _____

9. _____

10. _____

11. _____

12. What kind of boat do Inuits use in the summer? _____

13. Why don't they use those boats in the winter? _____

_____

1. Who met Tim at Crooked Lake? _____

2. Why were they surprised to see Tim?

_____

3. The first geese to greet Henry were his _____ .

4. Were Henry's children, grandchildren, and great grandchildren in the same flock as Henry? _____

5. In the winter, Henry gave the young geese practice in flying in a _____ .

6. The flocks started to fly north again in the month of _____ .

7. They did not arrive at Big Trout Lake until the month of _____ .

8. So it took them ▨ to make the trip north.
   - 2 or 3 months
   - 3 or 4 months
   - 5 months

9. After the flocks arrived at Big Trout Lake, _____ and the other young geese left the flock.

10. How old were all these geese? _____

11. Where did those geese move to? _____

12. What lake would this flock go to in the fall? _____

C REVIEW ITEM

The picture shows the sun and two balls. **Fix up the balls** so that half of each ball is in sunlight and half is in shadow.

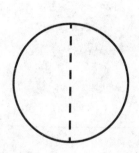

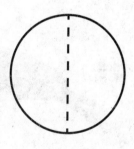

GO TO PART D IN YOUR TEXTBOOK

Label each animal in the picture below.

2. _____

1. _____

4. _____

3. _____

5. _____   6. _____

7.   Which animal in the picture is the biggest? _____

8.   Which animal in the picture is the smallest? _____

Write these words in the correct places on the map.

1. pebbled beach   3. summer home   5. ice floe   7. walruses

2. killer whales   4. path   6. seals

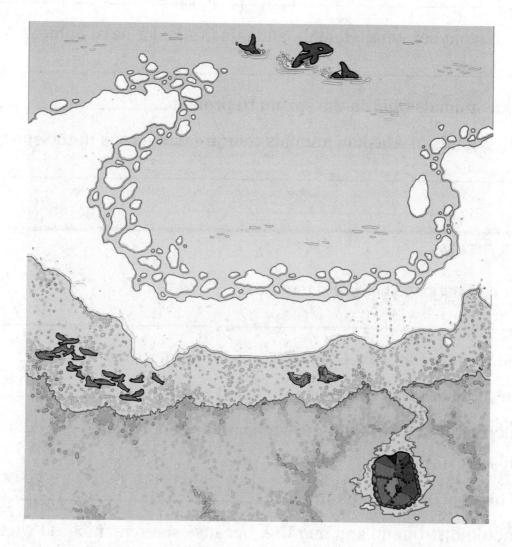

8. At the end of summer, the beach where Oomoo lived was different from the picture in 3 ways. What was different about the ice floe?

   _____

9. What was missing from the water? _____

10. What was missing from the beach? _____

GO TO PART E IN YOUR TEXTBOOK

A INFORMATION ITEMS

1. In what season are animals most dangerous in Alaska?

   _____

2. During what season do female animals in Alaska have babies?

   _____

3. Female animals fight in the spring to protect _____ .

4. Name 2 kinds of Alaskan animals that are dangerous in the spring.

   _____

B STORY ITEMS

1. What had happened to Usk's mother?

   _____

2. When Oomoo first saw Usk, Usk was no bigger than a _____ .

3. About how tall was Usk when he stood up now? _____

4. Oomoo's father said, "Full-grown bears are not ▮▮▮▮ ."
   • cubs   • pets   • dogs

5. Usk had become less playful last _____ .

6. Oomoo didn't run up and hug Usk because she remembered what
   _____ had told her.

7. What did Oolak throw at Usk? _____

8. Why did Oolak do that? _____

Scientists do not ignore ordinary things.

1. What word means that you don't pay attention to something?

    _____

2. What word tells about things that you see all the time? _____

3. What do we call highly trained people who study different things about

    the world? _____

Write these words in the correct places on the map.

1. ice floe   4. walruses   6. path

2. summer home   5. pebbled beach   7. seals

3. killer whales

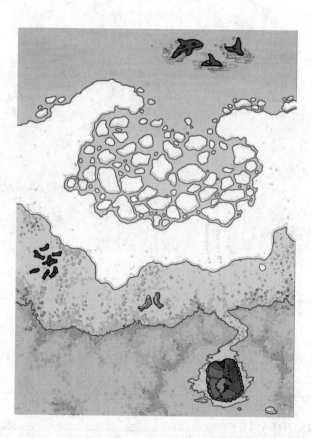

GO TO PART D IN YOUR TEXTBOOK

Name _____

_____

A INFORMATION ITEMS

1. What state is at the north end of the route on the map? _____

2. What country is at the south end of the route? _____

3. About how many miles is the route? _____

4. Write **OO** where Oomoo and Oolak lived.

5. Write **OH** where Old Henry lived in the summertime.

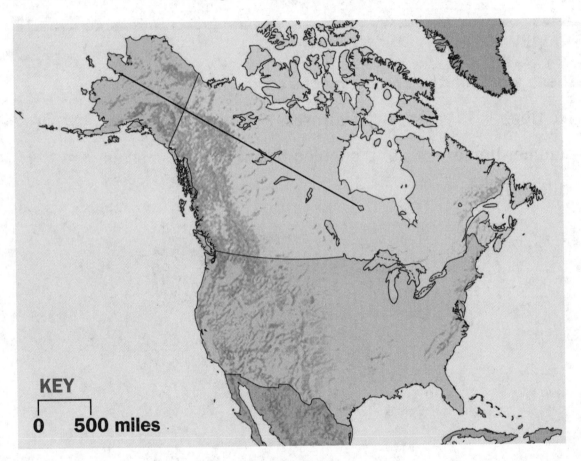

KEY

0   **500 miles**

B STORY ITEMS

1. What happened when Usk nudged Oolak with his nose?

_____

2. Usk started chasing Oomoo after _____

_____ .

3. When Usk caught up to Oomoo, he grabbed her ▮▮▮ .
  • boot   • collar

4. Then what did Usk do to Oomoo? _____

5. Who made the children stop playing? _____

6. When Oomoo reached her father, she didn't look at him. Why?

   _____

7. Will the father let the children play with Usk? _____

C REVIEW ITEMS

1. Write the missing seasons on the picture below.

2. Shade half of earth A and half of earth C.

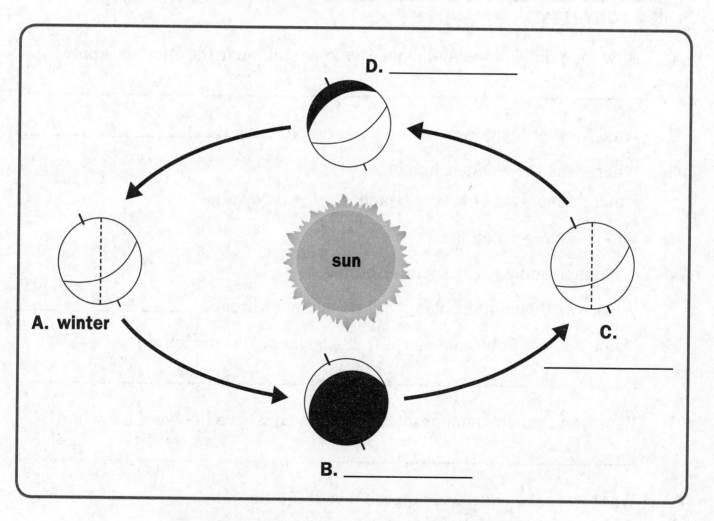

GO TO PART D IN YOUR TEXTBOOK

A PASSAGE 1 ITEMS

1. About how long are killer whales? _____

2. Compare the size of killer whales with the size of other whales. **Killer whales** _____ .

3. Are killer whales fish? _____

4. Are killer whales **warm-blooded** or **cold-blooded?** _____

5. Name 3 animals that are warm-blooded. _____

6. Name 3 animals that are cold-blooded. _____

B STORY ITEMS

1. How long did Oomoo and Oolak have to stay near the summer home?

   _____

2. What kind of home was the summer home? _____

3. Where was the summer home?
   • in a valley   • on the beach   • on a ridge

4. Which home was bigger?
   • summer home   • winter home

5. What was the only problem with the summer home? _____

6. Name 3 kinds of biting insects that Alaska has in the spring.

   _____

7. Why was Oomoo's summer home in a place where the wind blew hard?

   _____

8. What were the male seals on the beach fighting for?

   _____

9. What were the killer whales waiting for?

_____

10. What were Oomoo and her father in when the killer whales came close to them? _____

11. How many whales were there? _____

C SKILL ITEMS

Here are three events that happened in the chapter:

a. They were swarming by the thousands on the beach about half a mile from Oomoo's summer home.

b. Oomoo's father ordered Oomoo to stay near their summer home for two full days.

c. "I never want to be that close to killer whales again," she said to herself.

1. Write the letter of the event that happened near the beginning of the chapter. _____

2. Write the letter of the event that happened near the middle of the chapter.

_____

3. Write the letter of the event that happened near the end of the chapter.

_____

1. How many Great Lakes are there? _____

2. Color the Great Lakes on the map.

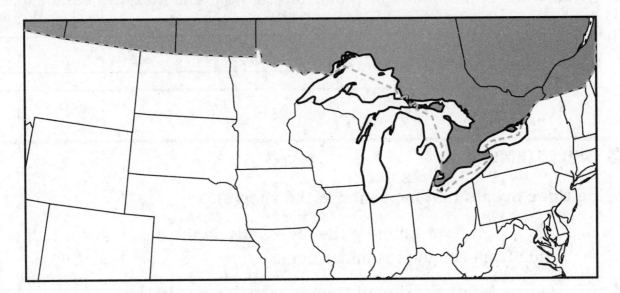

3. **Fill in the blanks to show the four seasons.**

winter, _____, summer, fall, _____, spring,

_____, _____.

GO TO PART E IN YOUR TEXTBOOK

A STORY ITEMS

Here are three events that happened in the chapter:

  a. During the winter, you can walk far out on the frozen ocean.

  b. But even if the killer whales didn't attack you, you would die within a few minutes after you went into the water.

  c. For a moment, Oomoo was going to say, "That's a pretty long way to drift."

1. Write the letter of the event that happened near the beginning of the chapter. _____

2. Write the letter of the event that happened near the middle of the chapter.

_____

3. Write the letter of the event that happened near the end of the chapter.

_____

4. During which season do ice floes start to melt? _____

5. During the winter in Alaska, you can walk far out on the ocean. Tell why.

_____

6. Do ice floes make noise in the winter? _____

7. Why do ice floes make noise in the spring?

_____

8. When Oomoo played on the ice floe in the spring, she could never go out to the end of the ice floe. What was at the end of the ice floe?

_____

9. Oomoo and Oolak were drifing on _____ .

10. You are out in the ocean on an ice chunk that melts. Name 2 ways you could die. _____

_____

11. Write **north, south, east,** and **west** in the boxes.

12. Make an **X** where the killer whales stay.

13. Make a **Y** on an ice chunk where Oomoo is not supposed to go.

14. Make a **Z** on the ice chunk Oomoo and Oolak are on.

15. **Make an arrow** from the **Z** to where they would go if the wind blows from the east. Show the path the ice chunk would follow.

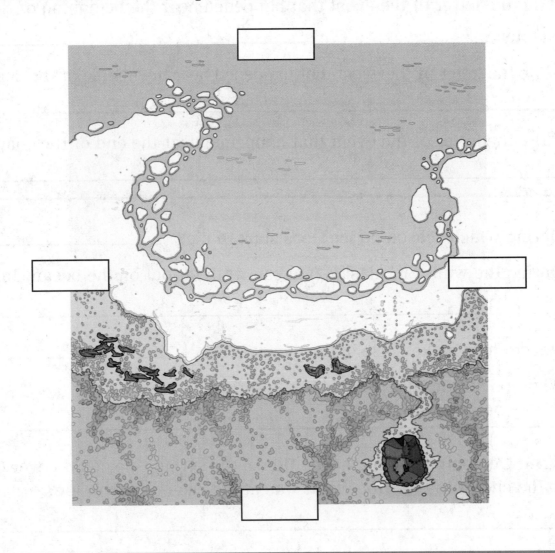

GO TO PART C IN YOUR TEXTBOOK

A INFORMATION ITEMS

1. Name 2 things that can make an ice chunk drift. _____

2. In which direction will you drift when you're in an ocean current?

   _____

3. In which direction will you drift when you're in a strong wind?

   _____

4. Write **north, south, east,** and **west** in the correct boxes.

5. In which direction is ocean current **A** moving? _____

6. In which direction is ocean current **B** moving? _____

7. Which direction is the wind coming from? _____

8. Make an arrow **above** ice chunk **C** to show the direction the current will move the ice chunk.

9. Make an arrow **above** ice chunk **D** to show the direction the current will move the ice chunk.

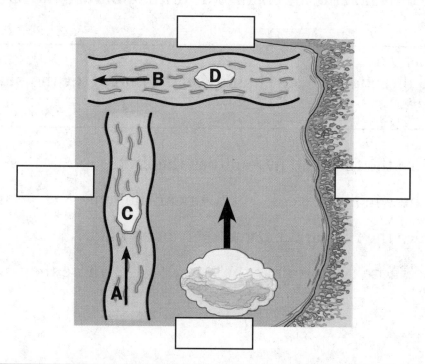

1. If you're out on the ocean and you spot a green cloud, what should you do?

   _____

2. What 2 things do those clouds bring?

   _____

3. Did Oomoo and Oolak follow the rule and about watching the sky?

   _____

4. Was the water **smooth** or **rough** where the wind hit the water?

   _____

5. How fast was the wind moving?

   _____

6. In which direction was the ice chunk headed?

   _____

7. Name the direction the ice chunk was drifting **before** the big wind came up.

   _____

8. Name the direction the ice chunk was drifting **after** the big wind hit it.

   _____

9. Where were the flies and mosquitoes thick?

   • where the wind was weak   • near the tent   • over the ocean

10. Where were the flies and mosquitoes not as thick?

    • near the shore   • near the tent   • where the wind was strong

11.   What did Oomoo and Oolak do to make the ice chunk rock?

_____

12.   Name 2 things that tell about the cloud that Oomoo saw.

_____

C REVIEW ITEMS

The picture shows the sun and two balls. Fix up the balls so that half of each ball is in sunlight and half is in shadow.

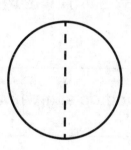  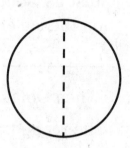

sun

GO TO PART D IN YOUR TEXTBOOK

A STORY ITEMS

1. The wind blew Oomoo and Oolak off course. In which direction were they drifting before the big wind blew? _____

2. In which direction did the big wind blow them? _____

3. When Oomoo heard Oolak's voice, she turned to look at him. Where was Oolak? _____

4. What did Oomoo put in the water to help Oolak? _____

5. Just as Oomoo was sliding off the ice chunk, a huge wave hit it. Where on the ice chunk did Oomoo and Oolak end up?

   _____

6. When Oolak asked Oomoo, "Are we going to die?" did Oomoo say what she really thought? _____

7. When the wind died down, rain and hail began to fall. Which made more noise, the **wind** or the **rain and hail?** _____

8. Which was colder, the **ocean water** or the **rain?** _____

9. How long did the rain come down hard?

   • 10 minutes   • an hour   • half an hour

10. At the end of the chapter, what did Oomoo see beyond the ice floe?

    _____

11. Did she tell Oolak what she saw? _____

12. Tell why. _____

13. After the big wind died down, Oomoo and Oolak shouted for help. Why couldn't anyone hear them? _____

    _____

14. Make an arrow from the **X** to the C-shaped ice floe. Show the path the ice chunk was supposed to follow.

15. Which letter shows where the ice chunk was at the end of today's chapter? _____

16. Which letter shows where the killer whales were? _____

17. Make an arrow from the **Q** to show which way the big wind blew.

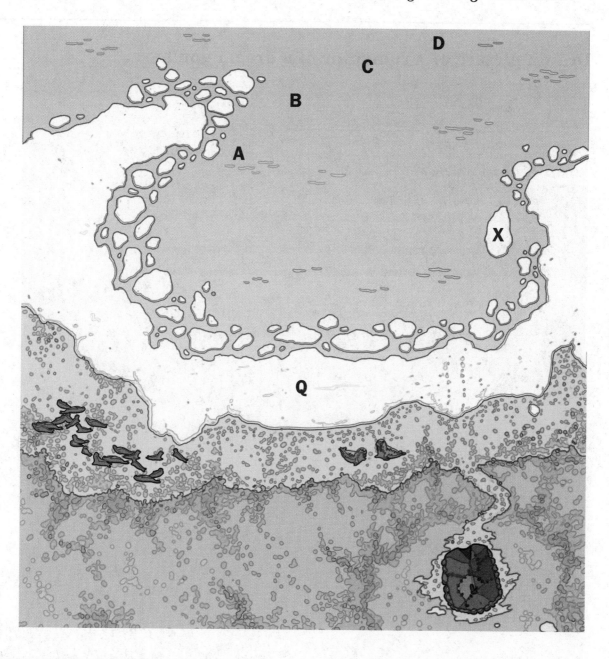

GO TO PART C IN YOUR TEXTBOOK

A POEM ITEMS

1. **Make up another part for the poem.**

    Hold fast to dreams

    _____

    _____

2. **Draw a picture of a runner or of a dream you have.**

1. What do we call literature that is true? _____

2. What do we call literature that is made up? _____

3. Name the 3 main ways that literature is presented.

   _____

4. The chapters about Henry and Tim are ▮▮▮▮ .
   • nonfiction   • fiction

5. The passage about the tilt of the earth is ▮▮▮▮ .
   • nonfiction   • fiction

6. The passage called Literature Types is ▮▮▮▮ .
   • nonfiction   • fiction

7. *Old Henry* is a ▮▮▮▮ .
   • play   • poem   • story

8. *Dreams* and *The Runner* are ▮▮▮▮ .
   • plays   • poems   • stories

END OF LESSON 20

A INFORMATION ITEMS

1. What are the clouds made of? _____

2. What kind of cloud does picture **A** show? _____

3. Write the letter of the clouds that may stay in the sky for days at a time. _____

4. Write the letter of the storm clouds. _____

5. Write the letter of the clouds that have frozen drops of water.

   _____

6. Write the letter of the clouds that may be five miles high. _____

7. Look at cloud **A.** At which number does a drop of water start? _____

8. What happens to the drop at the number **2?** _____

9. Draw 2 arrows on cloud **A** to show how a hailstone forms and returns to **1.**

A

B

C

10. If you break a hailstone in half, what will you see inside the hailstone? _____

11. The picture shows half a hailstone. How many times did the stone go through a cloud? _____

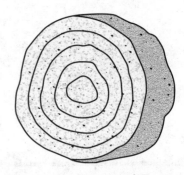

B STORY ITEMS

1. Oomoo slapped her boot on the ice to make noise. Why did she want the people on shore to hear the noise? _____

   _____

2. Why did she want the killer whales to hear the noise? _____

   _____

3. Was Oomoo sure that someone would hear her? _____

4. About how far was the ice chunk from the tent? _____

5. About how far was the ice chunk from the killer whales? _____

C REVIEW ITEMS

1. Write **north, south, east,** and **west** in the correct boxes.

2. In which direction is ocean current **J** moving?

   _____

3. In which direction is ocean current **K** moving?

   _____

4. Which direction is the wind coming from? _____

5. Make an arrow above ice chunk **L** to show the direction the current will move the ice chunk.

6. Make an arrow above ice chunk **M** to show the direction the current will move the ice chunk.

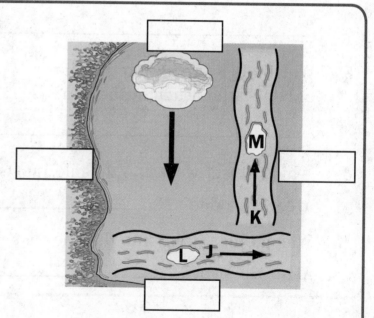

GO TO PART E IN YOUR TEXTBOOK

Look at the pile in the picture.

1. Things closer to the bottom of the pile
    went into the pile _____ .

2. Which object went into the pile **first?**

    _____

3. Which object went into the pile **last?**

    _____

4. Which object went into the pile
    earlier—the knife or the book?

    _____

5. Which object went into the pile
    earlier—the pencil or the cup?

    _____

6. Which object went into the pile **just
    after** the bone? _____

7. Which object went into the pile **just
    after** the pencil? _____

1. Oomoo and Oolak dug their heels into dents in the ice so that Usk could not _____ .

2. What did Oomoo see that scared her? _____

3. Why did Oomoo slap the ice with her hand?

   _____

4. While Oomoo and Oolak sat by the tent, they had to study

   _____ and _____ .

5. They had to do that so they would remember to look _____ .

6. Did Oomoo find out why the killer whale didn't attack Usk? _____

7. The people of the village formed a big ring. Who stood in the middle of the ring? _____

8. What did the women give Usk? _____

9. What did Oomoo's father paint on each side of Usk?

   _____

10. Why were Oomoo and Oolak so proud of Usk?

    _____

C REVIEW ITEM

Fill in the blanks to show the four seasons.

winter, _____ , summer, fall, _____ ,

spring, _____ , _____

GO TO PART D IN YOUR TEXTBOOK

Name _____

A INFORMATION ITEMS

1. Write the letter of the layer that went into the pile **first.** _____

2. Write the letter of the layer that went into the pile **next.** _____

3. Write the letter of the layer that went into the pile **last.** _____

4. Which layer went into the pile **earlier**—B or C? _____

5. Which layer went into the pile **earlier**—A or C? _____

6. Write the letter of the layer where we would find the skeletons of humans. _____

7. Write the letter of the layer that has dinosaur skeletons. _____

8. Write the letter of the layer where we find the skeletons of horses. _____

9. What's the name of layer C? _____

10. Write the letter of the layer we live on. _____

11. Are there any dinosaur skeletons in layer D? _____

12. Which came earlier on the earth, dinosaurs or horses? _____

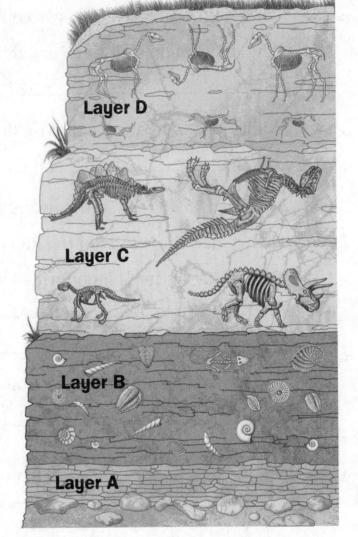

13. Which came earlier on the earth, strange sea animals or dinosaurs?

_____

14. What kind of animals lived in the Mesozoic? _____

1. Write the missing seasons on the picture below.

2. Shade half of earth **A** and half of earth **C**.

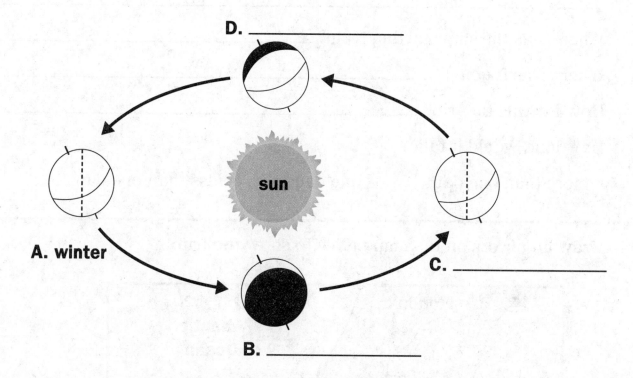

D. _____

sun

A. winter

C. _____

B. _____

Name _____

_____

INFORMATION ITEMS

1. How old was Edna Parker? _____

2. How did Edna usually feel on the ship?
   • happy   • bored   • fearful

3. Why wouldn't Edna be bored on this trip? _____

   _____

4. Where was the ship starting from? _____

5. Where was it going? _____

6. How far was the trip? _____

7. How long would it take?

   • more than one day   • one day   • less than one day

8. Draw an **arrow** on the map below to show the trip.

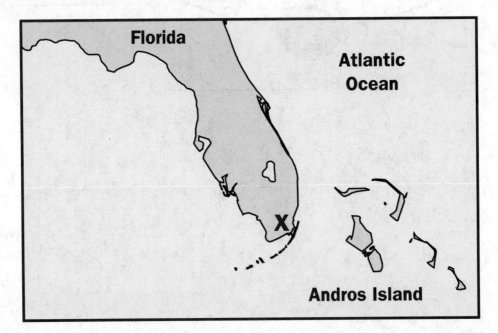

9. The ship would pass through a place where hundreds of ships have sunk or been lost. Name that place. _____

10. Circle the 3 things you find in the Bermuda Triangle.
    - huge waves
    - mountains
    - streams
    - whirlpools
    - sudden storms
    - ice floes

11. As the girls left the map room, Captain Parker told them to stay away from the sides of the ship and the _____ .

B REVIEW ITEMS

Look at the picture below.

1. Shade the part of the earth where it is nighttime.

2. Which side of the earth is closer to the sun, **A** or **B**? _____

3. Which side of the earth is in nighttime? _____

4. Which side of the earth is in daytime? _____

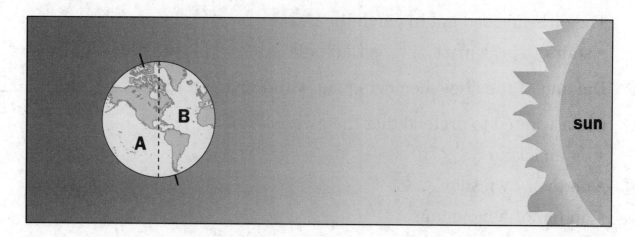

GO TO PART D IN YOUR TEXTBOOK

A INFORMATION ITEMS

1. How old was Edna Parker? _____

2. How did Edna usually feel on the ship?
   - happy   - bored   - tired

3. As the girls left the map room, Captain Parker told them to stay away

   from the _____ and the _____ .

4. Why didn't the girls stay in the galley?
   - The cook complained about his tooth.
   - It was dirty.
   - It smelled bad.

5. The girls didn't stay in the engine room because the engineer told them

   that they would have to ▮▮▮▮ .
   - go to the galley   - work   - sing

6. The girls decided not to climb the ▮▮▮▮ .
   - stairs   - mast   - flag pole

7. Did any of the crew members play with Edna and Carla? _____

8. Carla wanted to pretend that they were ▮▮▮▮ .
   - on an island
   - on their own ship
   - on top of a mountain

9. Which girl wanted to play in the lifeboat? _____

10. How many crew members were watching while Edna and Carla talked

    about playing in the lifeboat? _____

After Edna and Carla left the map room, they went to different places on the ship.

11. Write the letter that shows where they went just after they left the map room. _____

12. Write the letter that shows where they went next. _____

13. Write the letter that shows where they sat down in the sun. _____

B **REVIEW ITEMS**

1. How many Great Lakes are there? _____

2. Color the Great Lakes on the map.

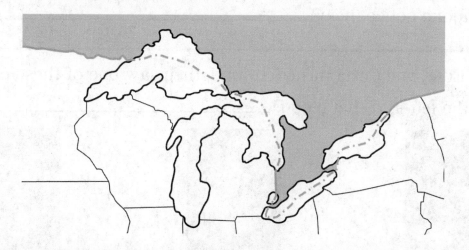

GO TO PART C IN YOUR TEXTBOOK

Name _____

1. When today's chapter began, Edna and Carla were pretending they had their own ship. Who was the captain? _____

2. Circle 3 things the first mate did to look more like a sailor.
   - took off her shoes
   - wore a sailor suit
   - wrapped a handkerchief around her head
   - wore short pants
   - rolled up her pants

3. What happened to the lifeboat when the girls were in it?
   - It dropped into the water.
   - It turned over.
   - It rang a bell.

4. What part of the lifeboat hit the water first, the bow or the stern?

   _____

5. What happened to Edna when the boat hit the water?
   - She fell out of the boat.
   - She bumped into Carla.
   - She hit her head.

6. What 2 things did the girls do to make the people on the large ship notice them? _____

   _____

7. Did anyone notice them? _____

8. When Edna and Carla turned around, they saw one of these clouds. Write the letter of that cloud. _____

A

B

C

9. When the girls started bailing, there was about _____ inches of water in the boat.

10. What made the girls top bailing?

    • a whirlpool   • a wind   • an airplane

11. At the end of the story, how high were the waves? _____

12. How fast were the winds moving? _____

B **REVIEW ITEMS**

1. In which direction do geese migrate in the fall? _____

2. In which direction do geese migrate in the spring? _____

3. Write the directions **north, south, east,** and **west** in the boxes.

4. Make a line that starts at the circle on the map and goes north.

5. If you start at the circle and move to the number **2,** in which direction do you go? _____

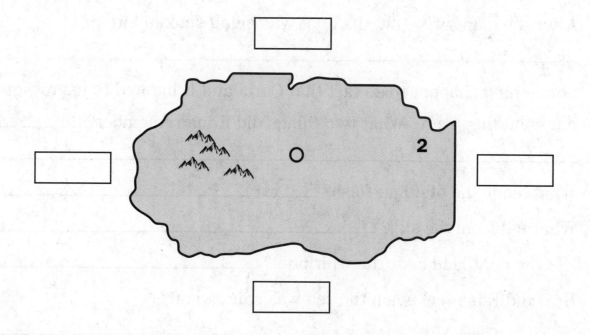

GO TO PART C IN YOUR TEXTBOOK

A INFORMATION ITEMS

1. Whirlpools are made up of moving _____ .

2. A whirlpool is shaped like a _____ .

3. What happens to something that gets caught in a whirlpool? _____

_____

B STORY ITEMS

1. What happened to the lifeboat when the girls got in it? _____

_____

2. When today's chapter began, Carla shouted that she saw land. What did
   she really see? _____

3. When could Edna see in the distance?

   • at the top of a wave   • at the bottom of a wave

4. After the giant wave hit, the boat was being sucked into a

   _____ .

5. Some things happened so fast that Carla and Edna had to try to figure
   out what they were. What two things did Edna remember? _____

   _____

6. What made the blinding flash? _____

7. What fell from the sky? _____

8. Did the boat land near the whirlpool? _____

9. How did Edna feel when the sea was calm again?

   _____

10. About how deep was the water when Edna stepped out of the lifeboat?

   _____

11. About how far was it from the lifeboat to the beach? _____

1. Write **north, south, east,** and **west** in the correct boxes.

2. In which direction is ocean current **P** moving? _____

3. In which direction is ocean current **Q** moving? _____

4. Which direction is the wind coming from? _____

5. Make an arrow next to ice chunk **R** to show the direction the current will move the ice chunk.

6. Make an arrow above ice chunk **S** to show the direction the current will move the ice chunk.

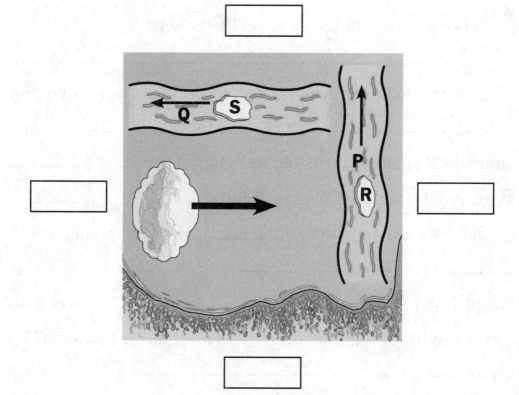

GO TO PART D IN YOUR TEXTBOOK

A   **STORY ITEMS**

1.   After the giant wave hit the boat in the last chapter, what was the boat
     being sucked into? _____

2.   Some things happened so fast that Carla and Edna had to try to figure
     out what they were. What made the blinding flash?

     _____

3.   What fell from the sky? _____

4.   About how far was it from the lifeboat to the beach?

     _____

5.   What was right behind the beach? _____

6.   What was strange about the sand on the beach?

     _____

7.   Edna and Carla woke up when it was dark. What woke them up?

     _____

8.   The animal Edna saw was as big as some of the _____ .

9.   Did the animal walk on **4 legs** or **2 legs**? _____

10. Where did the girls go to spend the last part of the night?

     _____

11. Did the girls get much sleep? _____

12. What was the first thing the girls discovered in the red sand?

     _____

13. The footprints were ▓▓▓▓ long.

     • a foot   • a yard   • half a meter

1. Write the letter of the earth that shows the person in daytime.

   _____

2. Write the letter of the earth that shows the person 6 hours later.

   _____

3. Write the letter that shows the person another 6 hours later.

   _____

4. Write the letter that shows the person another 6 hours later.

   _____

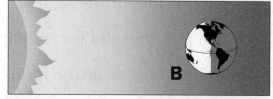

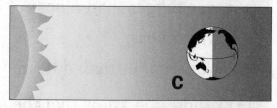

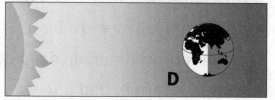

5. Which letter on the map shows Alaska? _____

6. Which letter shows Canada?

   _____

7. Which letter shows the main part of the United States? _____

8. Which 2 letters show where Inuits live? _____

9. How warm is it during winter in Alaska? _____

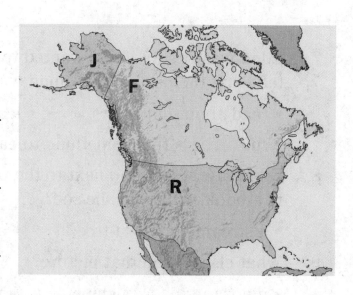

GO TO PART C IN YOUR TEXTBOOK

A STORY ITEMS

1. What was strange about the sand on the beach where Edna and

   Carla landed? _____

2. The footprints of the animal were _____ long.

3. How many toes did each footprint have? _____

4. What did the size of the footprints tell about the size of the animal?

   • It was bigger than a bear.

   • It was a bear.

   • It was smaller than a bear.

5. How did Edna know that the animal was very heavy?

   • The footprints were long.

   • The footprints made deep dents.

   • The footprints had 3 toes.

6. What part of the animal made the deep groove between the footprints?

   _____

7. Edna wasn't sure if she wanted to follow the animal. Circle 2 things that
   tell what the parts of her mind wanted to do.

   • read about dinosaurs   • learn more about the animal

   • run   • find something to eat   • think

8. Edna saw something next to the path that she recognized from a picture
   in a book. What did she see?

   • a stream   • a tree   • a bug

9. What else was in that picture?

   • dinosaurs   • ships   • rocks

10. How did that make her feel? _____

11. Write the letter of the footprint made by the heaviest animal. _____

12. Write the letter of the footprint made by the lightest animal. _____

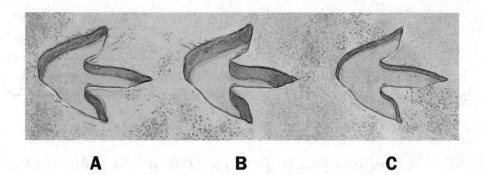

A   B   C

The picture shows marks left by an animal.

13. Make an arrow from dot **A** to show the direction the animal is moving.

14. Write the letter of the part that shows a footprint. _____

15. Write the letter of the part that shows the mark left by the
animal's tail. _____

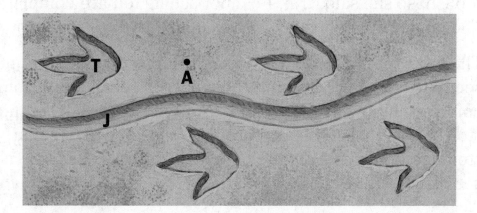

GO TO PART C IN YOUR TEXTBOOK

A **SETTING, CHARACTERS, PLOT**

Answer these questions about the story *The Emperor's New Clothes.*

1. What is the main setting for this story? _____

2. Name the main character in this story. _____

3. Circle the letter of the correct plot for this story.

   a. A thief sold a new suit to the emperor, a suit that no one could see. The thief said that only smart people could see the suit. Nobody wanted to look foolish, so everyone pretended they could see the suit. The emperor walked through the town completely naked. A child asked, "Why is the emperor naked?" Then everyone knew they had been fooled.

   b. A thief sold a new suit to the emperor, a suit that no one could see. The thief said only smart people could see the suit. The emperor's wife was one of the smartest people the emperor knew. He asked her if she could see the new suit. She was not afraid of looking foolish, so she said, "No, I cannot see it. You are completely naked!" The emperor laughed and ordered his guards to take the thief to jail.

   c. The emperor ordered a new suit for himself, a suit that no one could see. When he wore the suit, the emperor became invisible. No one could see him when he walked through the town. One night, a thief stole the suit while the emperor was sleeping. After that, the thief stole many things from the people of the town because no one could see him.

STORY ITEMS

1. Why did the emperor's palace have so many mirrors? _____

   _____

2. How many tailors spent all their time making clothes for the emperor?

   _____

3. The thief told the emperor that only the _____ people
   would be able to see the magic fabric he had.

4. Why didn't the emperor admit that he could not see the magic fabric?

   _____

5. How much did the emperor pay for his new suit of clothes?

   _____

6. Why didn't the empress say that the emperor was naked? _____

   _____

7. Why did the emperor have a parade?

   _____

8. Who finally asked why the emperor was naked? _____

9. What did the crowd do when people realized that the emperor
   was naked? _____

10. How did the emperor change after that day? _____

    _____

C AUTHOR'S PURPOSE

Match the author's purpose to each title. Circle **persuade, entertain**, or **explain**.

1.	How to Care for Wild Birds	persuade	entertain	explain
2.	Don't Vote for Sherman Brown	persuade	entertain	explain
3.	Molly's Magic Marble	persuade	entertain	explain
4.	Easy Way to Make Bread	persuade	entertain	explain
5.	Melvyn Goes to Bermuda	persuade	entertain	explain
6.	Why You Need a New Car	persuade	entertain	explain
7.	Growing Vegetables in Your Kitchen	persuade	entertain	explain
8.	How to Build a Tree House	persuade	entertain	explain
9.	10 Reasons for Not Eating Junk	persuade	entertain	explain
10.	Attack of the Pink Elephants	persuade	entertain	explain

D LITERATURE TYPES

Answer these questions.

1. What do we call literature that is made up? _____

2. What do we call literature that is true? _____

3. Name the 3 main ways that literature is presented. _____

_____

Finish the story with your partner or group.

Two years after the parade, a different thief came to the emperor's palace. The thief pretended to be a tailor. The thief told the emperor that he had a magnificent fabric that appeared to be invisible to fools.

_____

_____

_____

_____

_____

_____

END OF LESSON 30

A **STORY ITEMS**

1. Edna and Carla saw a winged animal. Was that animal a bird? _____

2. How do you know?

   • It had teeth.   • It didn't have a beak.   • It didn't have feathers.

3. Its wings were covered with something that looked like ▮▮▮▮ .

   • feathers   • leather   • hair

4. How long ago did those winged animals live on the earth?

   • a thousand years ago

   • a million years ago

   • a hundred million years ago

5. Circle the name of the dinosaur the girls saw.

   • Triceratops   • mammoth   • Tyrannosaurus

6. What cracked the tree that Edna was hiding behind?

   • Tyrannosaurus's head   • Tyrannosaurus's foot

   • Tyrannosaurus's tail

7. What happened to Edna when the tree cracked?

   _____

8. Before Edna started to run, she heard noises from the clearing. What made the leathery flapping sound?

   • Tyrannosaurus   • the flying dinosaur   • Carla

9. Whose bones were making the crunching sound?

   _____

10. Tyrannosaurus didn't hear Edna running because it was ▮▮▮▮ .

    • sleeping   • eating   • scratching

11. As Edna ran through the jungle toward the beach, what did she see on the path? _____

12. Did Edna slow down when she saw it? _____

13. When Edna got to the beach, she realized that something was wrong. What was wrong? _____

1. Write **north, south, east,** and **west** in the correct boxes.

2. In which direction is ocean current **F** moving? _____

3. In which direction is ocean current **G** moving? _____

4. Which direction is the wind coming from? _____

5. Make an arrow above ice chunk **H** to show the direction the current will move the ice chunk.

6. Make an arrow next to ice chunk **L** to show the direction the current will move the ice chunk.

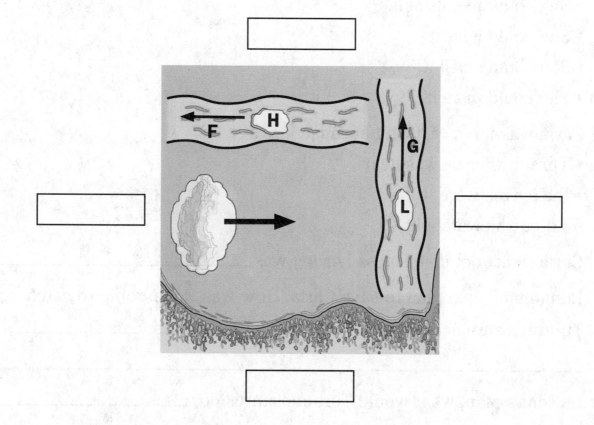

GO TO PART C IN YOUR TEXTBOOK

A STORY ITEMS

1. At the beginning of the chapter, Edna was trying to decide something. Circle what she was trying to decide.

   - whether she should go back into the jungle

   - whether she should hide under the boat

   - whether she should call for help

2. Edna didn't call to Carla because the sound would ▮▮▮▮ .

   - make the birds fly

   - not be loud enough

   - catch the dinosaur's attention

3. When Edna was near the clearing, she couldn't see Tyrannosaurus. Circle 2 ways she knew that Tyrannosaurus was nearby.

   - She could feel its skin.

   - She could hear it.

   - She could smell it.

   - She could taste it.

4. Carla was lying very still because ▮▮▮▮ .

   - Tyrannosaurus was near

   - the leaves were wet

   - Edna was watching

5. Carla didn't get up because her leg was _____ .

6. Edna made up a plan to save Carla. How was Edna going to catch

   Tyrannosaurus's attention? _____

   _____

7. In Edna's plan, what would Tyrannosaurus do? _____

   _____

8. What would Carla do? _____

    _____

9. Did Edna get to try her plan? _____

10. What came into the clearing when Tyrannosaurus was moving back
    and forth? _____

11. What were Edna and Carla trying to do at the end of the chapter?

    _____

B REVIEW ITEMS

1. What kind of boat do Inuits use in the summer? _____

2. Why don't they use those boats in the winter? _____

    _____

3. During which season do ice floes start to melt? _____

4. During winter in Alaska, you can walk far out on the ocean. Tell why.

    _____

5. Do ice floes make noise in the winter? _____

6. Why do ice floes make noise in the spring? _____

    _____

GO TO PART C IN YOUR TEXTBOOK

Name _____

INFORMATION ITEMS

1. What comes out of a volcano? _____

2. Draw arrows at **A**, at **B**, and at **C** to show the way the melted rock moves.

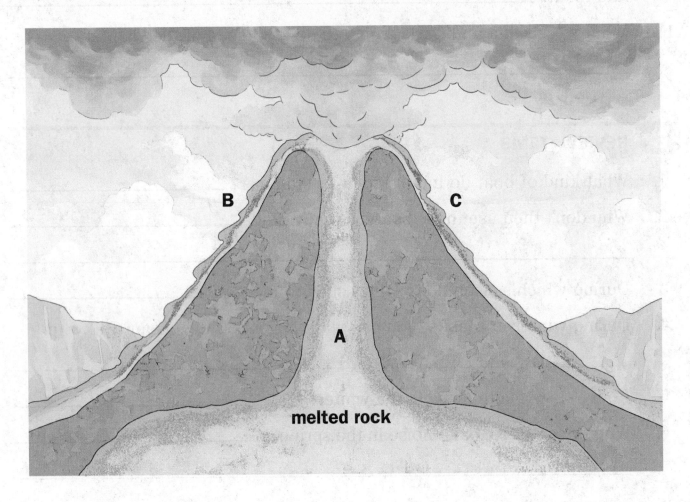

3. Two things happen to melted rock when it moves down the sides of a volcano. Circle those 2 things.

   • It gets hotter.

   • It gets cooler.

   • It hardens.

   • It runs faster.

   • It gets softer.

4. What is it called when the earth shakes and cracks? _____

B STORY ITEMS

1. When Edna was near the clearing in the last chapter, she couldn't see Tyrannosaurus. Circle 2 ways she knew that Tyrannosaurus was nearby.
   - She could taste it.
   - She could hear it.
   - She could feel its skin.
   - She could smell it.
2. What came into the clearing when Tyrannosaurus was moving back and forth? ______________________________
3. At the beginning of today's chapter, Tyrannosaurus was fighting ________ .
   - Triceratops
   - a mammoth
   - a flying dinosaur
4. Who do you think won the fight? ______________________________
5. What kept making the earth rock from side to side?
   - earthquakes
   - the volcano
   - the storm
6. What made the boiling cloud of smoke? ______________________________
7. Why did Edna fall down on the beach? ______________________________

   ____
8. When the girls were in shallow water, what formed underwater?

   ____
9. Who fell into the crack? ______________________________
10. What did the volcano do just after Edna got into the boat?

    ____
11. Did the girls know where they were going at the end of the chapter?

    ____

GO TO PART D IN YOUR TEXTBOOK

Name _____

A STORY ITEMS

1. What color was the water where it was shallow?

   _____

2. What color was the water where it was deepest?

   _____

3. Edna had blisters on her hands from _____ .

4. As the girls sat in the lifeboat, they could see a billowing cloud in the

   distance. What was making that cloud? _____ .

5. Name 2 kinds of supplies you'd need to stay on the ocean for a long time.

   _____

6. In which direction were the girls drifting? _____

7. Edna was thirsty. Why didn't she drink some ocean water?

   • It was warm.   • It was salty.   • It was dirty.

8. What made the boat move faster and faster?

   _____

9. While the lifeboat was in the whirlpool, why did the clouds seem to
   be spinning?

   • because of the wind.   • because the boat was spinning

                 • because Edna was sick

10. Did the girls know how they got out of the whirlpool? _____

11. The water in the bottom of the boat was very warm, so that water had
    been in the boat for ▓▓▓▓ .

    • a few seconds   • a few minutes   • a long time

12. After Edna woke up, she saw fish. What color was the water?

    _____

13. Why was Edna thinking about chewing on raw fish?
  • because she needed something salty
  • because she needed food
  • because she needed water

B **REVIEW ITEMS**

Draw arrows at **X**, at **Y**, and at **Z** to show the way the melted rock moves.

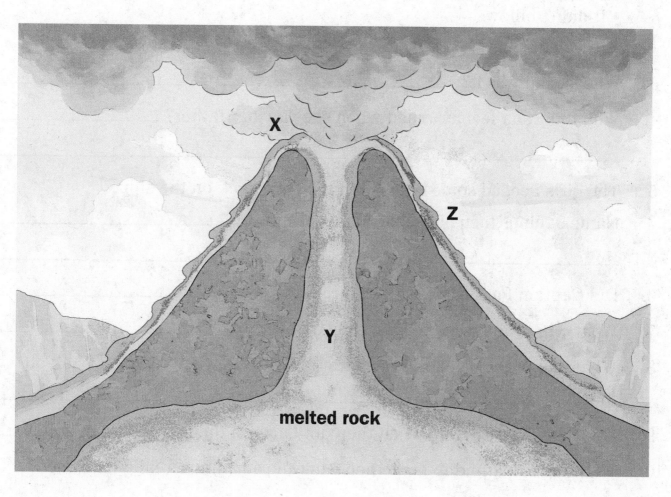

melted rock

GO TO PART D IN YOUR TEXTBOOK

Name _____

1. What did Edna see that told her a ship was in the distance?

   _____

2. How did she know it wasn't from the island?

   • It billowed.

   • It didn't billow.

   • It was black.

3. Whose ship was it? _____

4. Why did Edna feel ashamed when she saw her father? _____

   _____

5. The girls needed some care when they got back on the ship.

   Name 3 things they needed. _____

   _____

6. Did Captain Parker believe the girls' story? _____

7. What day of the week did the girls go overboard? _____

8. What day of the week did the girls think it was when they got back on

   the ship? _____

9. What day was it really when they got back on the ship? _____

10. What did Edna find to make her think the adventure really happened?

    _____

11. The sand in Edna's pocket must have come from _____ .

1. How long ago did dinosaurs live on the earth?

   _____

2. What is it called when the earth shakes and cracks? _____

3. Write the missing seasons on the picture below.

4. Shade half of earth **A** and half of earth **C.**

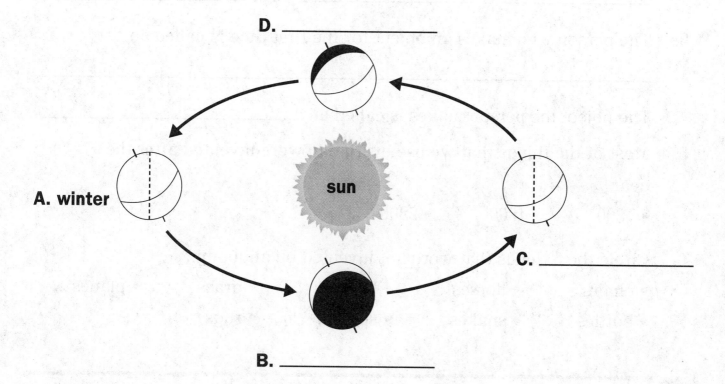

GO TO PART C IN YOUR TEXTBOOK

Name _____

1. Name 3 things that are made by humans. _____

_____

2. What is a person doing when the person makes an object for the first time?

_____

3. The person who makes an object for the first time is called an

_____ .

4. The object the person makes is called an _____ .

5. Most of the things that we use every day were invented after the

   year [   ] .

   • 1800   • 1900   • 2200

6. Circle the 5 things that were not invented by anybody.

   • chairs   • horses   • flowers   • grass   • planes

   • bottles   • snakes   • spiders   • rugs

1. Circle 2 reasons it was embarrassing to go places with Grandmother
   Esther.

   • She walked fast.   • She talked a lot.

   • She chewed gum.   • She mumbled to herself.

   • She talked loudly.

2. What did Grandmother Esther like to talk about?

   _____

3. Did she look at the displays of dinosaurs for a long time? _____

4. Circle 3 displays that Grandmother Esther wanted to see.

- radios
- cave people
- clothing
- airplanes
- horses
- automobiles

5. Grandmother Esther made a speech in the exhibit hall about the people who invented the airplane. How did Leonard feel?

_____

6. What did the other people in the exhibit hall do after the speech?

_____

C REVIEW ITEMS

1. Write the missing seasons on the picture below.

2. Shade half of earth **A** and half of earth **C**.

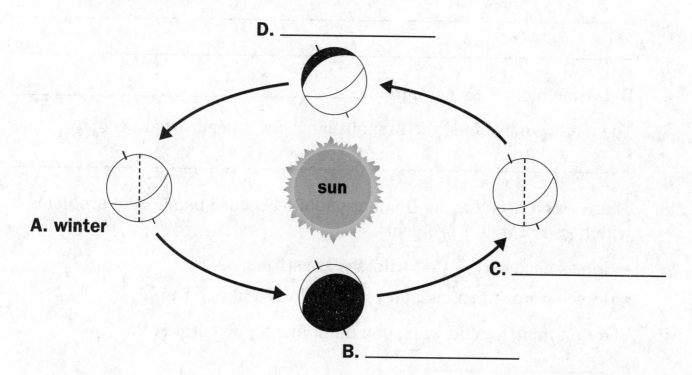

D. _____

A. winter

sun

C. _____

B. _____

GO TO PART D IN YOUR TEXTBOOK

A STORY ITEMS

1. What was wrong with the waterbed that Grandmother Esther invented?

   _____

2. What did Grandmother Esther's folding bike sometimes do when a person

   was riding it? _____

3. Circle 2 things that Grandmother Esther ate for lunch.
   - apple
   - egg
   - ice cream
   - cake
   - cookie
   - sandwich

4. Did Leonard know what he wanted to invent? _____

5. At first Leonard thought that he couldn't be an inventor because

   _____

   _____ .

6. Did Grandmother Esther agree? _____

7. The men who invented the first airplane saw a need. What need?

   _____

8. There was a need for the first automobile because people had problems
   with horses. Circle 2 problems.

   - Horses need care.
   - Horses are strong.
   - Horses weren't fast enough.
   - Horses like to run.

9. The first thing you do when you think like an inventor is find

   a _____ .

10. What's the next thing you do?
    - Ask questions.
    - Meet the need.
    - Go to a museum.

1. Draw arrows at **J,** at **K,** and at **L** to show the way the melted rock moves.

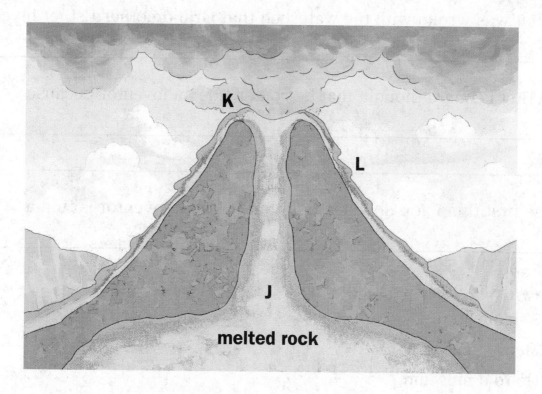

melted rock

2. What is a person doing when the person makes an object for the first time? _____

3. The person who makes an object for the first time is called an _____ .

4. The object the person makes is called an _____ .

GO TO PART C IN YOUR TEXTBOOK

A STORY ITEMS

1. What was wrong with the waterbed that Grandmother Esther invented?

   _____

2. At first Leonard thought that he couldn't be an inventor because

   _____

   _____ .

3. The first thing you do when you think like an inventor is find a

   _____ .

4. What's the next thing you do?
   • Ask questions.
   • Meet the need.
   • Go to a museum.

5. Leonard's father had two ideas for inventions. One was something that cut down on traffic. What was his other idea?

   _____

6. Did Leonard's father think like an inventor? _____

7. Leonard's mother had an idea for an invention. What was it?

   _____

8. Had Grandmother Esther heard that idea before? _____

9. Did Grandmother Esther like hearing about that? _____

10. Did Leonard get any good ideas for inventions by talking to people?

    _____

11. What did Leonard think the hardest part of being an inventor was?

    _____

1. How many Great Lakes are there? _____

2. Color the Great Lakes on the map.

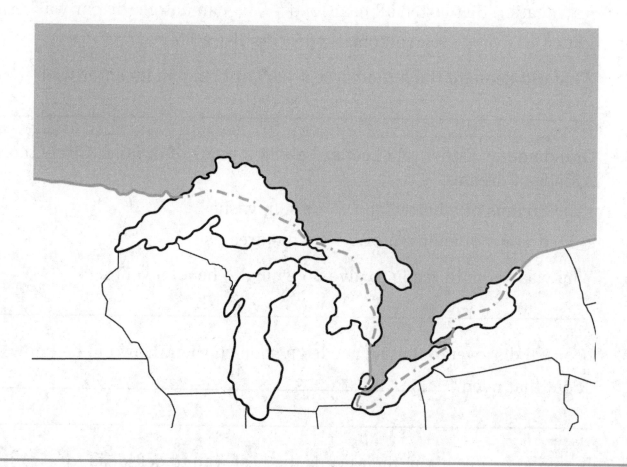

3. The picture below shows the sun and two balls. Fix up the balls so that half of each ball is in sunlight and half is in shadow.

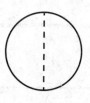  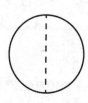

sun

GO TO PART C IN YOUR TEXTBOOK

A STORY ITEMS

1. Leonard's mother had an idea for an invention. What was it?
    - a vacation that lasted all year long   • an automatic car washer
                    • an automatic grocery list writer

2. What did Leonard think the hardest part of being an inventor was?

    _____

3. Grandmother Esther told Leonard about 2 kinds of dreams. Circle those 2 kinds of dreams.
    - the dreams of a butterfly   • silly wishes
    - the dreams of an inventor   • daydreams

4. Why was Leonard ready to give up trying to be an inventor?

    _____

5. Leonard discovered that he needed a shoe checker. How did he know

    about that need? _____

    _____

6. Is asking people about their needs the best way to get ideas for

    inventions? _____

7. The best way to think like an inventor is to do things. When you do

    things, you look for _____ that you have.

B REVIEW ITEMS

1. In which direction do geese migrate in the fall? _____

2. In which direction do geese migrate in the spring? _____

3. Write the directions **north, south, east,** and **west** in the boxes.

4. Make a line that starts at the circle on the map and goes north.

5. If you start at the circle and move to the number **4,** in which direction do you go? _____

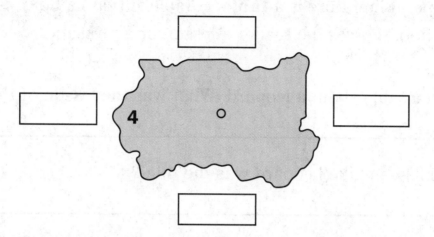

6. Shade the part of the earth where it is nighttime.

7. Which side of the earth is closer to the sun, **A** or **B?** _____

8. Which side of the earth is in nighttime? _____

9. Which side of the earth is in daytime? _____

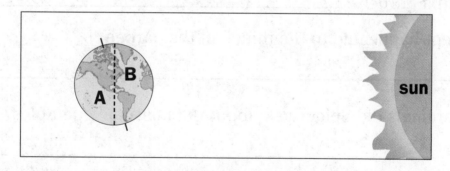

10. **Fill in the blanks to show the four seasons.**

winter, _____ , summer, fall, _____ ,

spring, _____ , _____

GO TO PART C IN YOUR TEXTBOOK

A FABLES

Fables

One type of literature is a **fable.** A fable is fiction, but it is a special kind of fiction. It gives the reader a lesson or a message.

1. You read a fable about a leopard. What was the lesson of that fable?

   _____

2. Why did it seem like Leopard was the thief?

   _____

3. Who was really the thief? _____

B STORY ITEMS

1. At the beginning of this story, what was unusual about how the leopard

   looked? _____

2. Who had a garden? _____

3. What kept happening to the things in the garden?

   _____

4. Which animals did Spider ask about the missing vegetables?

   _____

5. Who had a plan to find out who was taking the vegetables? _____

6. Who really took things from the garden? _____

7. How did Deer trick Leopard into going to the garden?

   _____

8. What happened to Leopard when he got there?

_____

9. How did that change Leopard?

_____

10. From that day on, which two animals were no longer friends?

_____

C SETTING, CHARACTERS, PLOT

1. What is the main setting for this story? _____

2. Name the 3 main characters in this story.

_____

3. Which passage tells the plot for this story? _____

   a. Deer, Leopard, and Spider ate dinner together every night at Spider's house. Spider had a big garden, but a thief was stealing some of the vegetables. One night, Deer, Leopard, and Spider set a trap for the thief. They waited all night, but the thief didn't come. Leopard was so tired, he forgot where the trap was and fell into it. A fire in the trap made black spots all over Leopard.

   b. Someone was taking vegetables from Spider's garden. Deer said it wasn't him. Leopard said it wasn't him, either, but the vegetables kept disappearing from Spider's garden. Deer told Spider how to set a trap for the thief. Then, Deer led Leopard into the trap. First, Spider believed Leopard was really the thief. Then, Spider and Leopard realized it had to be Deer. A fire in the trap made black spots all over Leopard.

   c. Deer, Leopard, and Spider ate dinner together every night at Spider's house. Spider had a big garden, but a thief was stealing some of the vegetables. Deer told Spider how to set a trap for the thief. The next night, Deer tripped over a log and fell into the trap. A fire in the trap made black spots all over Deer.

Name _____

A **STORY ITEMS**

1. When Leonard did things like washing the car, what did he pay
   attention to? _____

2. Each problem told Leonard about something he could
   _____ to solve the problem.

3. How long did Leonard try to find different problems?

   _____

4. What invention did he think would solve the problem he had with eggs?

   _____

5. What problem did Leonard have with his clothes at bedtime?

   _____

6. What invention did he think could solve that problem?

   _____

7. What invention did Leonard think could solve the problem he had when
   it rained? _____

8. What problem did Leonard have when he washed his dog?

   _____

9. Which invention did Leonard's mother think he should make?

   _____

10. Did Grandmother Esther name an invention that Leonard should

    make? _____

REVIEW ITEMS

1. The first thing you do when you think like an inventor is find a

   _____ .

2. What's the next thing you do? _____

   _____

---

3. Write **north, south, east,** and **west** in the correct boxes.

4. In which direction is ocean current **W** moving? _____

5. In which direction is ocean current **X** moving? _____

6. Which direction is the wind coming from? _____

7. Make an arrow above ice chunk **Y** to show the direction the current will move the ice chunk.

8. Make an arrow next to ice chunk **Z** to show the direction the current will move the ice chunk.

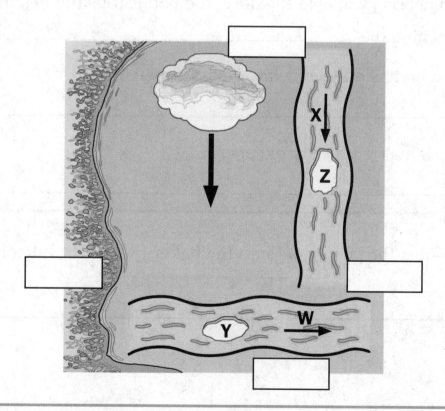

GO TO PART C IN YOUR TEXTBOOK

A **STORY ITEMS**

1. Circle the reasons that people in the street thought Grandmother Esther was mad at Leonard.

   - She made faces.
   - She pointed her finger.
   - She talked softly.
   - She talked loudly.
   - She kicked cats.

2. What invention did Leonard think could make his grandmother talk in a softer voice? _____

3. What would the invention do when Grandmother Esther talked louder?

   _____

Grandmother Esther explained how the electric eye works.

4. When somebody walks in the door, the body stops the beam of light from reaching the _____ .

5. When the body stops the beam, what happens?

   _____

6. What does that tell the shopkeeper?

   _____

---

7. Why couldn't the people get into the bakery while Grandmother Esther talked?

   _____

8. What did those people say about Grandmother Esther's talk?

_____

9. How did Leonard feel? _____

10. Will the buzzer in the bakery make noise for picture **A** or picture **B**? _____

11. What's the name of the invention shown in the pictures?

_____

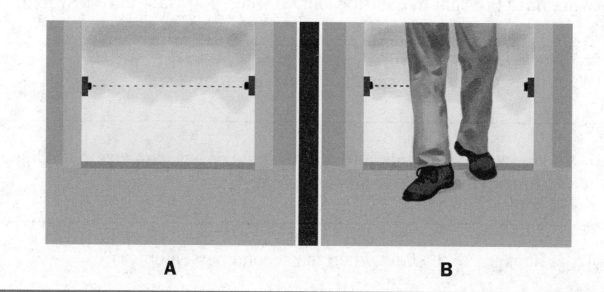

A   B

B **REVIEW ITEMS**

1. What color are all geese when they are born? _____

2. What's the name of geese that are all white? _____

3. What's the name of geese that are black, brown, and white?

_____

GO TO PART C IN YOUR TEXTBOOK

A STORY ITEMS

1. Leonard got his idea for a great invention when Grandmother Esther told him to do something. What did she tell him to do?

_____

Leonard's first invention had problems.

2. What does the light in a dark room do when you walk into the room?

_____

3. What does the light do when you leave the room?

_____

4. Let's say two people walk into a dark room. What happens to the light in the room when the first person enters?

_____

5. What happens to the light when the second person enters?

_____

6. What will Leonard use to make the lights work automatically?

_____

7. Did Leonard's mother understand how his invention would work?

_____

8. Grandmother Esther told Leonard that every invention has

_____.

9. So what does the inventor have to do?

• quit   • solve the problems   • hide the problems

Here's the rule about an electric eye: **Each time the beam of light is broken, the light changes.** Shade the bulbs that are off for each problem. The first problem is already done for you.

10. The light is off. The beam is broken 4 times.

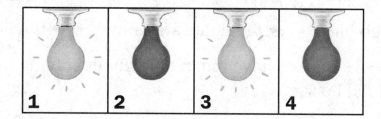

Is the light **on** or **off** at the end? _____

11. Here's another problem. The light is off. The beam is broken 8 times.

a. Shade the bulbs that are off.

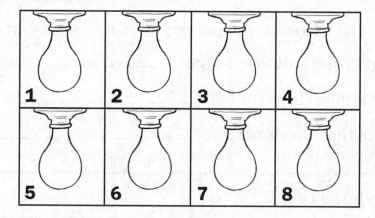

b. Is the light **on** or **off** at the end? _____

12. Here's another problem. The light is off. The beam is broken 3 times.

a. Shade the bulbs that are off.

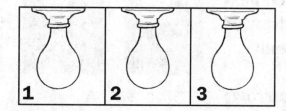

b. Is the light **on** or **off** at the end? _____

GO TO PART C IN YOUR TEXTBOOK

Name _____

STORY ITEMS

1. At the beginning of today's chapter, Leonard was trying to solve this problem. When a second person goes into the room, ▮▮▮ .

    • the lights go on   • the lights stay on   • the lights go off

2. Leonard saw a sign that gave him a clue about solving his problem. What kind of sign did he see?

    _____

3. His invention had to know whether a person was moving ▮▮▮ .

    • in or out   • fast or slow   • now or later

4. So how many beams does a doorway need? _____

5. If a person moves **into** the room, which beam will be broken first—the **inside beam** or the **outside beam**? _____

6. Which beam will be broken next? _____

7. Will the lights turn **on** or **off**? _____

8. The picture shows two electric eye beams on the side of each door. The number **1** shows the beam that is broken first. The number **2** shows the beam that is broken next. On each picture, draw an arrow to show which way the person is moving. The first arrow is already drawn.

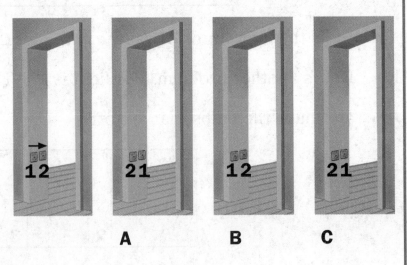

A   B   C

Here's the rule about an electric eye. **Each time the beam of light is broken, the light changes.**

9. a. The light is off. The beam is broken 3 times. Shade the bulbs that are off.

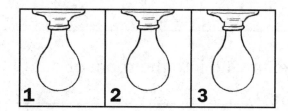

   b. Is the light **on** or **off** at the end? _____

10. a. The light is off. The beam is broken 6 times. Shade the bulbs that are off.

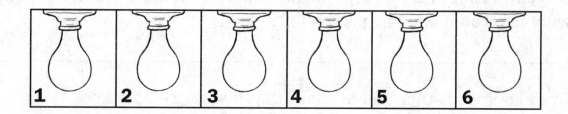

   b. Is the light **on** or **off** at the end? _____

11. a. The light is off. The beam is broken 5 times. Shade the bulbs that are off.

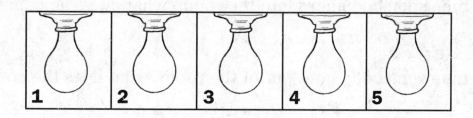

   b. Is the light **on** or **off** at the end? _____

GO TO PART C IN YOUR TEXTBOOK

A STORY ITEMS

1. In the last chapter, Leonard saw a sign that gave him a clue about solving his problem. What kind of sign did he see?

   _____

2. Would a person be moving into the room or out of the room if the **inside** beam is broken first? _____

3. Which way would a person be moving if the **outside** beam was broken first?

   _____

4. Leonard's first idea had a problem. What would happen if three people were in a room and one person left?

   _____

5. Grandmother Esther told Leonard that his device could not

   _____ .

6. Letting water out of the sink gave Leonard an idea about his counter. What number did his counter have to count to? _____

7. Every time somebody goes into the room, what does the counter do?

   • +1   • −1   • 0

8. Every time somebody goes out of the room, what does the counter do?

   • +1   • −1   • 0

9. What number does the counter end up at when the last person leaves the room? _____

10. What happens to the lights when the counter is at zero?

    _____

The solid arrows show people going into the room. The dotted arrows show people leaving the room. For each picture, circle the word that tells about the lights in the room.

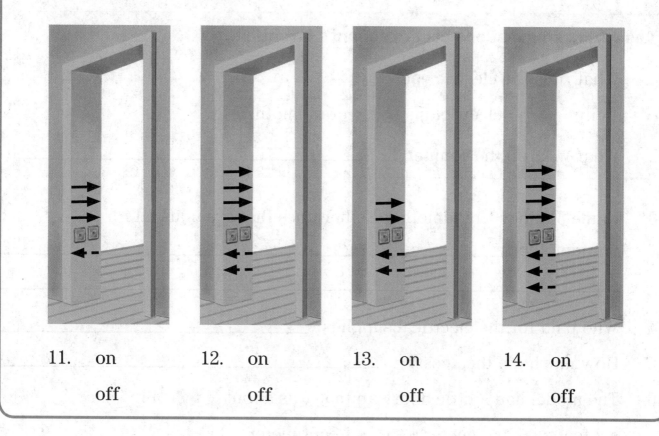

11. on

off

12. on

off

13. on

off

14. on

GO TO PART C IN YOUR TEXTBOOK

A STORY ITEMS

Answer these questions about Leonard's invention.

1. What runs the electric eye?

   • city   • electricity   • grandmothers

2. What will run the counter? _____

3. Name 3 things Grandmother Esther does that are unusual for a grandmother. _____

   _____

4. Who paid for the electrical supplies? _____

5. How much did they cost? _____

6. The model had a little doorway that was about ▨▨▨ tall.

   • 2 feet   • 1 meter   • 1 centimeter

7. There was a _____ connected to the top.

8. The light is off. A doll goes through the doorway. What happens to the light if the outside beam is broken first?

   _____

9. Did Leonard's device work? _____

10. Did he test it more than 1 time? _____

11. What does an inventor get to protect an invention?

    _____

12. If other people want to make copies of an invention, they have to make a deal with the _____ .

13. What does the inventor usually make those people do?

    _____

14. Special lawyers who get protection for inventions are called ▭ .

    • patents   • doctors   • patent attorneys

15. How many meetings did Leonard and Grandmother Esther have with a
    special lawyer? _____

16. How much money did Grandmother Esther pay the lawyer?

    • 3 thousand dollars   • 3 hundred dollars   • 1 thousand dollars

B **REVIEW ITEMS**

Use these names to answer the questions: **Tyrannosaurus, Triceratops.**

1. What is animal **P?** _____

2. What is animal **J?** _____

GO TO PART C IN YOUR TEXTBOOK

Name _____

A   STORY ITEMS

1. On which table would Leonard set up his display? _____

Look at the picture below. Not all the spaces have numbers and letters.

2. **Fill in the letters** that go at the top of each aisle.

3. **Number** all the tables in the aisle where Leonard's display was.

4. **Circle** Leonard's table.

5. Leonard and his grandmother started where the **X** is. They first went across the hall to the correct aisle. Then they walked down that aisle to their table. **Draw a path** that shows how they went from the **X** to their table.

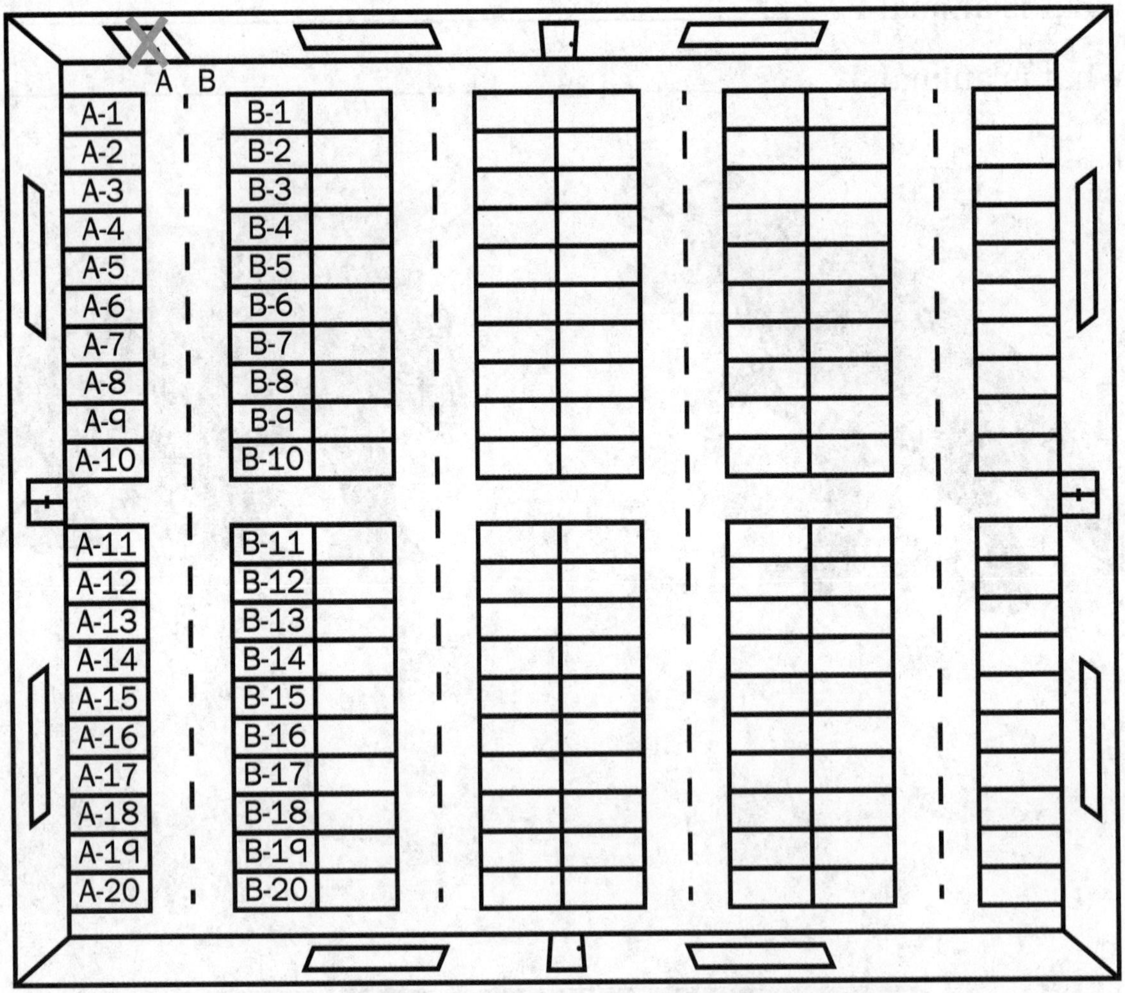

6. **Circle** Leonard's table.

7. What space is just north of Leonard's space? _____

8. What space is just west of Leonard's space? _____

9. What space is just south of Leonard's space? _____

10. What space is just east of Leonard's space? _____

North

A-1		B-1	C-1		D-1	E-1		F-1	G-1		H-1
A-2		B-2	C-2		D-2	E-2		F-2	G-2		H-2
A-3		B-3	C-3		D-3	E-3		F-3	G-3		H-3
A-4		B-4	C-4		D-4	E-4		F-4	G-4		H-4
A-5		B-5	C-5		D-5	E-5		F-5	G-5		H-5
A-6		B-6	C-6		D-6	E-6		F-6	G-6		H-6
A-7		B-7	C-7		D-7	E-7		F-7	G-7		H-7
A-8		B-8	C-8		D-8	E-8		F-8	G-8		H-8
A-9		B-9	C-9		D-9	E-9		F-9	G-9		H-9
A-10		B-10	C-10		D-10	E-10		F-10	G-10		H-10

West — **East**

A-11		B-11	C-11		D-11	E-11		F-11	G-11		H-11
A-12		B-12	C-12		D-12	E-12		F-12	G-12		H-12
A-13		B-13	C-13		D-13	E-13		F-13	G-13		H-13
A-14		B-14	C-14		D-14	E-14		F-14	G-14		H-14
A-15		B-15	C-15		D-15	E-15		F-15	G-15		H-15
A-16		B-16	C-16		D-16	E-16		F-16	G-16		H-16
A-17		B-17	C-17		D-17	E-17		F-17	G-17		H-17
A-18		B-18	C-18		D-18	E-18		F-18	G-18		H-18
A-19		B-19	C-19		D-19	E-19		F-19	G-19		H-19
A-20		B-20	C-20		D-20	E-20		F-20	G-20		H-20

South

GO TO PART C IN YOUR TEXTBOOK

A STORY ITEMS

1. Leonard was very disappointed when the fair opened. Tell why.

   • Lots of manufacturers showed up.

   • Not many people showed up.

   • Grandmother Esther talked too much.

2. How many people stopped at Leonard's display the first afternoon?

   _____

3. How many of them seemed very interested? _____

4. Why don't smart manufacturers act interested in the inventions that they want?

   • so they don't have to pay as much for the invention

   • because they are at the fair all day long

   • because they want to pay more for the invention

5. After supper, there were great crowds of people at the fair. Were these

   people manufacturers? _____

6. Did these people act interested in Leonard's invention? _____

7. Name 2 things that make you think the slim woman in the gray coat was a manufacturer.

   _____

   _____

8. Why would manufacturers want to make their deals before the prizes are announced?

   • so they could go home earlier

   • so they wouldn't have to pay as much

   • so they had something to do

9. Grandmother Esther gave 2 reasons that the manufacturers did not wait until the afternoon to make their deals. What are those 2 reasons?

_____

_____

Look at the picture below.

10. Make an **I** by each inventor.

11. Make an **M** by each manufacturer.

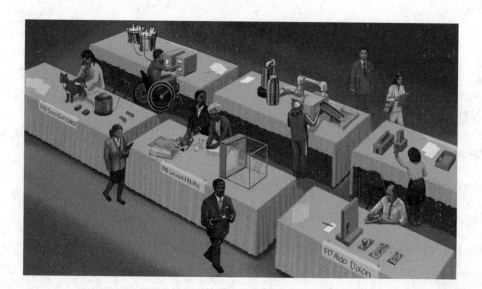

GO TO PART C IN YOUR TEXTBOOK

A **STORY ITEMS**

1. Leonard was very disappointed when the invention fair opened. Tell why.

   _____

2. Grandmother Esther gave 2 reasons that the manufacturers did not wait until Saturday afternoon to make their deals. What are those 2 reasons?

   _____

   _____

Look at the list of deals below.

3. **Underline** the best deal for an inventor.

4. **Circle** the best deal for a manufacturer.

   - 18 thousand dollars and 6 dollars for every copy sold
   - 12 thousand dollars and 6 dollars for every copy sold
   - 17 thousand dollars and 6 dollars for every copy sold

5. The slim woman in the gray coat said that not many people would be interested in Leonard's invention. Does she really think that?

   _____

6. Why did she say it?
   - She didn't want to talk to her boss.
   - She didn't want to pay a lot for the invention.
   - She didn't like the invention.

7. Why didn't Grandmother Esther want Leonard to make deals?
   - because he didn't know how
   - because he was too young
   - because he was too tired

8. The man with the slim woman wanted to make his company sound good to Leonard and Grandmother Esther. Tell why.

_____

_____

_____

9. Did his talk trick Grandmother Esther? _____

10. Which prize did Grandmother Esther think Leonard's invention would get?

_____

11. Let's say a manufacturer had not made a deal for an invention. Which would the manufacturer have to pay more money for, an invention that won a prize or an invention that did not win a prize?

_____

12. What lie did Grandmother Esther tell the bald man?
   • ABC Home Products is not interested.
   • ABC Home Products wants to make a deal.
   • ABC Home Products has too many inventions.

13. When Grandmother Esther told a lie, Leonard was going to remind her

that ABC Home Products _____

_____ .

GO TO PART C IN YOUR TEXTBOOK

A **SETTING, CHARACTERS, PLOT**—*Boar Out There*

1. What is the main setting for this story? _____

2. Name the main character in this story. _____

3. Write the plot for this story. Tell what everyone was afraid of. Tell what happened to Jenny in the woods. Tell how her feelings changed.

_____

_____

_____

_____

_____

_____

B **STORY ITEMS**—*Boar Out There*

1. Where were the people in Glen Morgan afraid to go?

_____

2. Why were they afraid?

_____

3. Who went into the woods? _____

4. How was the boar different from the way Jenny imagined him?

_____

_____

5. What did she do while the boar was near her?

_____

6. What scared the boar away? _____

7. Why did Jenny feel sorry for the boar? _____

_____

C **STORY ITEMS—*Little House on the Prairie***

1. What kind of vehicle did the family travel in? _____

2. The family came from the ▮▮▮▮ of Wisconsin.

   • Great Lake   • Big Woods   • Big City

3. In which direction were they going? _____

4. What did Pa do to the wagon to prepare it for crossing the creek?

_____

5. Jack was their _____ and Pet was one of their two

_____ .

6. How was Jack supposed to get across the creek? _____

7. Who jumped into the water in the middle of the creek? _____

8. Who drove the wagon the rest of the way? _____

9. Who was missing when the family got to the other side? _____

10. What did they think must have happened to him? _____

11. How many people did they see after they crossed the creek? _____

END OF LESSON 50

Fact Game Scorecard Sheet

Fact Game for Test 1

1	2	3	4	5
6	7	8	9	10
11	12	13	14	15
16	17	18	19	20

Fact Game for Test 2

1	2	3	4	5
6	7	8	9	10
11	12	13	14	15
16	17	18	19	20

Fact Game for Test 3

1	2	3	4	5
6	7	8	9	10
11	12	13	14	15
16	17	18	19	20

Fact Game for Test 4

1	2	3	4	5
6	7	8	9	10
11	12	13	14	15
16	17	18	19	20

Fact Game for Test 5

1	2	3	4	5
6	7	8	9	10
11	12	13	14	15
16	17	18	19	20

Thermometer Chart

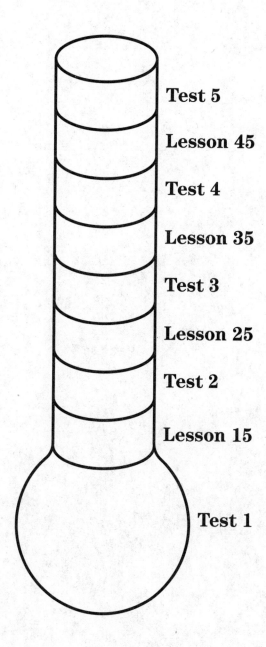

Test 5

Lesson 45

Test 4

Lesson 35

Test 3

Lesson 25

Test 2

Lesson 15

Test 1